British Airc
the Falklands War

LEE CHAPMAN

HISTORIC MILITARY AIRCRAFT SERIES, VOLUME 13

Front cover: Handley Page Victor ZM715 during a fast taxi run at Bruntingthorpe Aerodome.

Back cover: Westland Wasp XT787 of the Westland Wasp Historic Flight performs at the Midlands Air Festival in Falklands War colours.

Title page image: Westland Wasp HAS (Helicopter Anti-Submarine) Mk 1 XT787 (G-KAXT) painted in Falklands War camouflage colour scheme.

Contents page image: Westland Wessex HU5 (Helicopter Utility Mark 5) XT761 flies over HMS *Heron*. (Yeovilton Fleet Air Arm Base)

Author's note

For the purpose of this book, the term 'British aircraft' refers to any aircraft used by the British forces during the time of the conflict. Although most aircraft featured were designed and developed in the UK, it also includes aircraft that are not of British design or origin but were used by British forces, such as the MacDonald Douglas Phantom. The book is illustrated with modern images taken by the author that feature the aircraft types as they are now, including a guide to where they can be seen in the UK. Where possible, genuine Falkland War survivors have been pictured, but, where this was not possible, every attempt has been made to use images of the correct mark of aircraft. Where it fits the narrative, additional aircraft are featured to demonstrate the development or current status of these aircraft types. Occasionally, where there were no alternatives available, different marks of aircraft are featured for illustrative purposes – this is clearly identified throughout the book.

For further information please see www.chappersphotography.co.uk

Published by Key Books
An imprint of Key Publishing Ltd
PO Box 100
Stamford
Lincs PE19 1XQ

www.keypublishing.com

The right of Lee Chapman to be identified as the author of this book has been asserted in accordance with the Copyright, Designs and Patents Act 1988 Sections 77 and 78.

Copyright © Lee Chapman, 2022

ISBN 978 1 80282 242 7

Typeset by SJmagic DESIGN SERVICES, India.

Contents

Preface

Iremember going to Cosford Air Show as a child in the late 1980s; we went for a family day out. My dad was fascinated by aviation and dragged us all along. I do not remember much about the day, but I do remember the Avro Vulcan displaying. I am not sure if it was the noise of the thunderous jet engines, the sight and smell of those Smokey engines or the shadow cast by the giant flying tin triangle that captured my imagination, but it must have left an impression. I did not think about it much, and, for a long time, I lived firmly outside the world of aviation. Suddenly, around 20 years later, for want of something to do, I called my dad and said, 'Fancy going to Cosford this year?' He was thrilled and surprised and jumped at the chance.

It proved to be the beginning of something. For the next few years, my father and I would attend as many airshows as we could, specifically to see Vulcan XH558. Over time, a love for all historic aviation would grow, but, at first, there was only the Vulcan. The sight of the huge bomber passing over head never failed to impress. To me, it looked futuristic, even in the 21st century when it was over 50 years old. Even now, there is nothing like it in the skies – it is unique and when you add in the sound of the mighty Vulcan Howl, it just blows you away.

Through the rebirth of Avro Vulcan XH558 as a flying aircraft, my father and I were able to learn more about its role in the Falklands campaign and through this I was introduced to the world of aviation. The retaking of the Falklands required far more than just the Vulcan – a whole range of incredible, iconic aircraft contributed; it is also, arguably, the last conflict in which a largely

This image of Avro Vulcan XH558 was taken by my father, Keith Chapman.

British-built force of aircraft saw action. This book covers all the types of aircraft that contributed to Operation *Corporate* (the mission to retake the Islands). On a personal level, the grounding of the last flying Vulcan and the retirement of many iconic British aircraft such as the Harrier, Victor, Sea King and Nimrod seems to have been underlined by my father's untimely passing. It is with him in mind that I have produced this book, going through the images has brought back many happy memories, and I know he would have loved it.

Acknowledgements

I would like to thank the following organisations for permission to use copyright material in this book: Yorkshire Air Museum, The Fleet Air Arm Museum, The Avro Heritage Museum, the Army Flying Museum, Solent Sky Museum, Midlands Air Museum, RAF Cosford, RNAS Yeovilton, East Midlands Aeropark, the Imperial War Museum and the RAF Museums for permissions to photograph their exhibits on their sites. Every attempt has been made to seek permissions for copyright material and photographic rights in this book. However, if we have inadvertently used materials without permission we apologise, and we will make the necessary correction at the first opportunity.

I would also like to thank the team at Key Publishing; Georgia Massey for encouragement, motivation and support; Andy 'Loopy' Forester and Daniel Gooch for joining me on aircraft photography adventures. I would also like to acknowledge the support of my close family, especially my father, who was with me when many of these images were taken but sadly passed away in 2020. Finally, I would also like to acknowledge the hard work of airshow organisers, warbird operators, restorers, conservators, re-enactors and museum curators that keep the memories alive.

Chapter 1
Introduction

An ongoing dispute between the Argentine and British governments over the ownership of a group of islands in the South Atlantic reached boiling point when a group claiming to be Argentine scrap metal merchants raised the Argentine flag on South Georgia (a British territory roughly 850 miles southeast of the Falkland Islands). This act is now considered the first offensive action of the conflict. The Royal Navy quickly despatched its nearest asset, the ice patrol vessel HMS *Endurance*, in response.

Foreseeing a large-scale response from British forces, the Argentine government quickly ordered Operation *Rosario*, and, on 2 April 1982, undertook an amphibious invasion of the Falkland Islands, South Georgia and the South Sandwich Islands. Sir Rex Hunt was the Falkland Islands' governor at the time, and, because of the Islands' remote location, he had only limited forces to call upon. There were 69 Royal Marines present on the Islands and an additional civilian reserve, of which only 27 reported for duty. Despite brave resistance by the limited defending forces, the Islands were quickly captured and occupied by the Argentine commandoes.

Careful consideration had to go into the planned retaking of the Islands, which were over 8,000 miles from the British mainland. What assets were ready, available and able to make such a journey and operate effectively?

Victor K2 tankers were required to provided air-to-air refuelling to most aircraft en route to the South Atlantic. Handley Page Victor K2 XM715 is seen here during a recent fast taxi run at Bruntingthorpe.

The RAF's Hawker Siddeley Nimrods were amongst the first aircraft to arrive on Ascension Island to undertake reconnaissance of the area. Nimrod R1 XV249 also conducted search and rescue missions during the war.

On 31 March 1982, Prime Minister Margret Thatcher confirmed that a full-scale task force would be sent to retake the Islands. Admiral Sir Jon Fieldhouse took overall command directing the operations via satellite from the Fleet Operations Room in Northwood, London. Within the theatre itself, Admiral John 'Sandy' Woodward took charge. Aerial operations were overseen by Air Marshal Sir John Curtiss, who also remained in London to co-ordinate the effort. The South Atlantic task force consisted of over 30,000 personnel, almost 130 naval vessels and around 250 aircraft from the Fleet Air Arm (FAA), Army Air Corp (AAC) and Royal Air Force (RAF). The undertaking became known as Operation *Corporate*.

British air power was going through a transitional period as many aircraft types, such as the iconic Avro Vulcan, were due to be retired, whilst newer aircraft such as the Panavia Tornado were still in the training and evaluation phase. Compared to the Avro Vulcan, the Tornado is a very different design. It was configured for modern warfare with protection of UK and NATO operations in mind. No one foresaw the invasion of the Falklands and as such the requirements for retaking a remote, isolated archipelago had not been factored into the defence plans for the UK. Whilst it would go on to achieve great things, the new multi-role Tornado did not initially have the capabilities for a long-range bombing run. The remaining Vulcans would be given one last swansong.

The British task force faced a logistical nightmare; there were over 8,000 miles between the Falklands and the British mainland. Meanwhile, the coast of mainland Argentina was just over 400 miles away, giving the Fuerza Aérea Argentina (Argentine Air Force, FAA) a distinct home advantage. In addition, the terrain and climate of the remote Islands were uniquely demanding for any military operation. In order to successfully retake the Islands, Britain would first need to transport ships, men, aircraft, ammunition, vehicles and supplies to the area.

Fortunately, a remote volcanic island and British territory called Ascension Island was located approximately halfway between Britain and the Falklands. During the 1920s, a single runway, known as Wideawake Airfield, was installed there to assist transatlantic military and civilian logistics. At 10,000ft, the runway was just about long enough for the take-off and landing of the largest aircraft in the British fleet at the time.

A recently restored Panavia Tornado GR1 at RAF Cosford. Although newly in service at the time, the Tornado was not selected for action in the South Atlantic.

This is Avro Vulcan XH558. Despite their imminent retirement, a handful of Vulcans were selected to serve in the campaign.

Many of the resources required could be transported by sea to the well-located haven of Ascension, but the journey time via ship was over a week. Large transport aircraft, such as the C-130 Hercules and Vickers VC10, proved vital in their role of moving equipment and personnel across the Atlantic at speed. At around 8–10 hours via air, the journey time to Ascension was considerably faster than by ship.

Lockheed C-130 Hercules pictured recently at RAF Brize Norton. The American-designed aircraft is currently still in service with the RAF.

A Vickers VC10 at the RAF Museum, Cosford. The type retired from RAF service in 2013.

Falklands veteran Westland Wessex XT482 is seen here at the Fleet Air Arm Museum.

Although Wideawake Airfield had a 10,000ft runway, there was no parallel taxiway, and hard standing space to park aircraft around the airfield was severely limited. Storing and moving aircraft, helicopters and equipment was a supreme challenge in logistics. Additionally, there were no port facilities other than a single Jetty. Although ships could anchor nearby, helicopters such as the Westland Wessex proved vital in ferrying men and resources to and from the land efficiently.

At the end of the 1970s, the larger British Aircraft carriers, such as HMS *Ark Royal*, were decommissioned in favour of more cost effective, smaller ships with limited deck space. The Royal Navy was therefore no longer able to operate its larger fast jets. The flexibility offered by a helicopter that could take off and land vertically posed many advantages over fixed wing aircraft. When the fleet made its way towards the South Atlantic, helicopters were crammed into every space available. Even *Atlantic Conveyor*, a requisitioned Cunard cargo ship, contained six Wessex and four Chinook helicopters. Fortunately, one of the Chinooks was airborne when the vessel was hit by two Exocet AM39 missiles and sunk. The remaining Chinook landed safely on HMS *Hermes* and served with distinction throughout the rest of the conflict.

The modern RAF still operates a large fleet of upgraded Boeing Chinook helicopters.

Apart from aircraft designed as long-range airliners, such as the Vickers VC10, most of the RAF, AAC and FAA aircraft were not capable of reaching the South Atlantic without either a lift on an aircraft carrier or support from air-to-air refuelling aircraft. Whilst other aircraft including the VC10s were converted into tanking aircraft, most of the air-to-air refuelling work was carried out by the Handley Page Victor. The Lockheed Hercules aircraft were given additional fuel tanks and became the first propeller-driven aircraft in service with air-to-air refuelling probes. These modifications enabled the transports to deliver essential supplies and equipment to the South Atlantic.

The Handley Page Victor was one of the three V-bombers developed during the 1950s; like the Avro Vulcan, it was nearing the end of its operational career but had found a new lease of life as a tanker. The third V-bomber was the Vickers Valiant, which had long since ceased operations at the time of the Falklands War. Following its work in 1982, the Victor would continue in service for another ten years after the Falklands campaign and would even see action in the first Gulf War.

In 1982, the British military was undergoing a reduction in resources following the 1981 Defence Review. The Royal Navy was particularly hard hit and was forced to give up its largest aircraft carriers. Even HMS *Hermes*, the largest of the two available aircraft carriers at the time, was due for imminent retirement. However, when the Falklands were invaded, *Hermes* was back in favour and became the flagship of the British Fleet. Although still a capable ship, it was far from perfect. Its deck space was not sufficient to successfully operate supersonic fighters such as the F-4 Phantom effectively. *Hermes* also lacked the catapults and arrester hooks required to operate supersonic jets at their fully armed and fuelled maximum weights.

The British task force were therefore dependent on its fleet of subsonic V/STOL (vertical/short take-off and landing) aircraft: the Hawker Siddeley/British Aerospace (BAe) Harrier (the initial

Handley Page Victor K2 XL231, now at Yorkshire Air Museum. XL231 was involved in retraining crews for air-to-air refuelling in the build-up to the conflict and served in the air bridge role during the war.

Falklands veteran BAe Sea Harrier FRS1 XZ493 at the Fleet Air Arm Museum.

Harrier GR3 XZ991 at RAF Cosford.

Harriers were designed and built by Hawker Siddeley, which became a founding component of BAe in 1977). During the Falklands campaign, the Royal Navy operated its purpose-built Sea Harrier FRS1 variant in an almost constant combat air patrol over the task force. Every available Sea Harrier was sent to the conflict. Additionally, British Aerospace was encouraged to finish any on the production line as quickly as possible. More Harriers were still required and, as such, the RAF hastily adapted its GR3 Harriers to operate from the decks of the navy's carriers. These RAF aircraft were mainly operated in a ground-attack role during the war, as their radar and electronics were not optimised for operations over sea.

The famous Avro Vulcan was designed to deliver Britain's nuclear weapons. It was operational in the RAF from 1956, initially as a high-altitude bomber, but as the demands of the cold war shifted, it was switched to a low-level bomber. Avoiding retirement, the remaining ageing Vulcans were quickly deployed to Ascension Island to undertake the *Black Buck* bombing raids. At the time, these missions were the longest bombing runs in history, the success of which ensured the reputation of the Vulcan, which today remains one of the most revered aircraft ever developed in Britain.

On 1 May 1982, the first *Black Buck* mission took place. After an issue with the intended lead aircraft (Vulcan XM598), XM607 (pictured here) flew low level for almost 4,000 miles to successfully drop its bombs on Port Stanley airfield. One direct hit ensured that the runway was left unsuitable for the operation of Argentine fast jets, which certainly made life easier for the British landing forces. The raids were supported by Handley Page Victor K2 tankers, which met the Vulcan at various stages on the journey, demonstrating incredible logistical planning and navigation.

Avro Vulcan XM607 is seen being towed into the hangar for restoration, but it will be back on display in time for the 40th anniversary of its famous mission.

Chapter 2

The Logistical Challenge: Fixed Wing Transport Aircraft

T he RAF's transport division was one of the hardest working teams during the conflict; even during peacetime, transport aircraft are constantly in our skies. During any worldwide crisis, the transport aircraft of the RAF are always in the thick of the action. The modern-day fleet was busy collecting medical supplies during the COVID-19 pandemic, for example. In 1982, this was no different; however, a change in strategy and budget cuts had seen a reduction in the capabilities of Britain's aerial transport abilities. This decision was tied in with the changing nature of British overseas interests and the development of the Commonwealth of Nations. Self-rule for most former British colonies meant that Britain no longer retained the same interests in far-flung locations and, as such, the aerial transport strategy was based around supporting NATO and protecting the UK mainland. When these decisions were made, it seems that nobody envisioned an invasion of the remote Falkland Islands.

At the time, no serving aircraft could reach the Falklands without refuelling. Even the huge distances between the UK mainland and Ascension Island caused complications for the RAF. Most missions to

A Lockheed Hercules C-130K Mk 3 at the RAF Museum Cosford.

Lockheed Hercules XV202 C-130K Mk 3 on public display in the UK at the RAF Museum Cosford.

supply the area involved fuel stops at Gibraltar and on the west coast of Africa, in locations such as Dakar in Senegal. Air-to-air refuelling was not widely practised in all branches of British air power prior to this conflict. When Argentina invaded the Falklands, there was suddenly a great need and aircraft like the Hercules were quickly modified to take on fuel whilst in flight.

Before the British retaking of the Falkland Islands could be attempted, it was essential to ensure that there were enough men, firepower and resources within the area. Whilst some cargo would be sent via sea, air travel was by far the fastest means of transport. The first action was to set up a forwarding base on Ascension Island. On 2 April 1982, the first four RAF Hercules aircraft departed Lyneham for Gibraltar and so began the Hercules' contribution to Operation *Corporate*. An air bridge between the UK and Ascension was quickly established, where up to 16 flights a day would resupply Wideawake Airfield with key Army, RAF and Royal Navy personnel and essential supplies and equipment. Nos 24 and 30 squadrons concentrated on this air bridge and, throughout the conflict, were busy ferrying people and cargo.

Initially, the RAF ordered 66 C1 Hercules, which made up the bulk of the fleet in 1982, but these had a limited capacity. The C1 Hercules' cargo holds would usually be full long before the aircraft had reached its maximum take-off weight. Fortunately, these were already in the process of being upgraded and, by March 1982, 12 of the original C1s had been 'stretched', i.e., given a longer fuselage to create the new C3 variant. These were much more capable aircraft and had 37 per cent more cargo space and, as such, were able to carry more equipment. However, the bulk of the work during the conflict was undertaken by the C1s. Both variants were upgraded to take on fuel in flight and some aircraft were given underwing radar warning pods.

The Lockheed Martin C-130 Hercules was developed in the United States during the 1950s. Its first flight was in 1954 and, just two years later, it began to enter service with the United States Air Force. It is one of the most widely used transport aircraft of modern times and has seen extensive service with

Two modern day Lockheed Martin C-130J Hercules aircraft in formation for the RAF100 flypast over London in 2018. The size difference between the modern day C4 (stretched) and C5 give some idea of how the C1 and C3 would have compared.

air arms all over the world. During the Falklands campaign, it was one of the few aircraft types used by both sides, with the Argentine Air Force attempting risky overnight resupply missions with their Hercules aircraft throughout the war.

Amongst many duties, the RAF Hercules aircraft from Nos 47 and 70 squadrons were also responsible for resupplying the Naval task force whilst at sea. In order to achieve this, a series of airdrops took place. An airdrop involved the transport aircraft flying to the edge of the total exclusion zone to meet the task force and parachute down various supplies, equipment or personnel. The missions were dangerous, long and often required specially modified aircraft with extra long-range fuel tanks. Each Hercules airdrop mission mounted from Ascension was given a female name as code; the names progressed in alphabetical order mission by mission. By the time Port Stanley Airfield was liberated on 26 June 1982, they were up to 'V' for 'Violet', demonstrating how busy the fleet were on these tasks alone. Additionally, the Hercules aircrew from No 47 Squadron were also trained for covert special operations duties.

Below and opposite: Re-enactor Jed Jaggard brings the RAF Museum's Hercules to life, recreating how operations would have looked at the time.

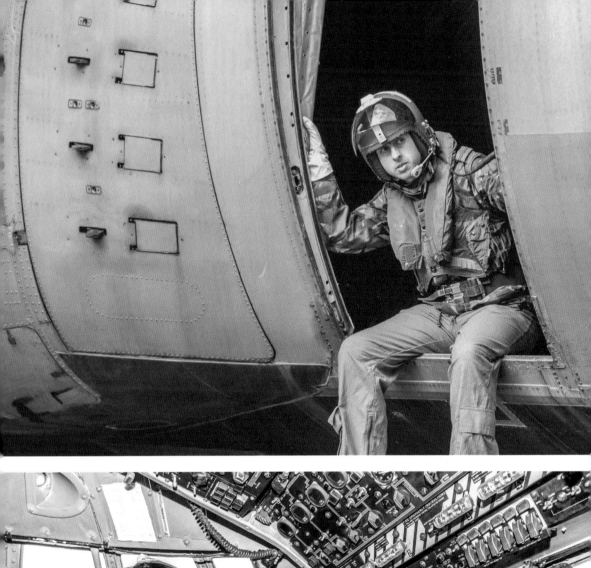

The example pictured above and below (XV202) is the only preserved Hercules on display in the UK. It was built at the Lockheed factory in Marietta, Georgia, US, and delivered to the RAF in 1967. It was delivered as a C1 but, in 1981, was 'stretched' into C3 configuration. It was one of only 12 C3 Hercules aircraft available for action at the start of the war. This aircraft was involved in the air bridge operations. Flight Lieutenant (Flt Lt) Ruston is known to have flown XV202 on a return resupply flight from Dakar two days before the Argentine surrender. XV202 served with the RAF until 2011, when it was delivered directly to the RAF Museum at Cosford, where it remains on external display.

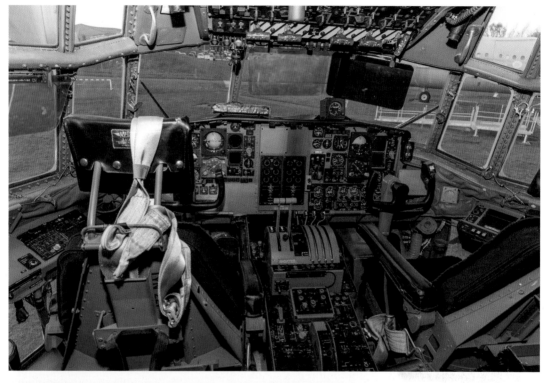

Above and left: Internal shots of the RAF Museum's Hercules C-130K Mk 3 XV202.

In the UK, the Hercules has been a reliable, rugged workhorse for over 50 years. In the mid-1960s, the RAF was looking for a tactical transport to replace its Blackburn Beverley aircraft. Although British manufacturers put forward some innovative and groundbreaking designs, they were deemed too ambitious and too expensive, and the decision was made to purchase an off-the-shelf Hercules direct from the US. The first C-130K models arrived in the UK in December 1967, where they were fitted with British avionics, radios and an air delivery system to safely release loads via parachute.

By the end of the campaign, the RAF Hercules aircraft had carried out over 50 airdrop sorties and over 600 air bridge flights between the UK and Ascension. The type had flown over 1,300 hours by the time of the Argentine surrender on 14 June 1982. The adaptability of the Hercules between roles enabled it to provide an invaluable service during the campaign. It was not initially designed with maritime operations in mind and, at the start of the campaign, could not take on board fuel in flight. By the end of the conflict, it was seeing use in numerous roles from cargo transport, airdrops, paratrooper drops and, shortly after the war, was even transporting VIPs like Prime Minister Margaret Thatcher, who visited the islands for four days in 1983.

Forty years later, the RAF still operate several Hercules aircraft, although after serving since 1967, they are due for imminent retirement from British service. The current aircraft are C-130J variants, which come in C4 (long fuselage) and C5 (shorter fuselage) designations. Although the type has been much upgraded since 1982, the role remains the same; they still offer tactical air transport support to the British forces and movement of cargo, supplies and troops. On 5 April 2018, the last RAF Hercules returned to RAF Brize Norton from RAF Mount Pleasant, the RAF's permanent base on the Islands since 1985. They had maintained over 36 years of continued service in the South Atlantic. The Hercules aircraft have now been replaced by the RAF Airbus Atlas.

Airbus A400M Atlas ZM417.

Modern-day Lockheed Martin C-130J C4 Hercules at RAF Brize Norton.

The Vickers VC10 was designed by Vickers-Armstrong at Brooklands, in Surrey, as a medium-capacity jet airliner. It was designed to be fast and efficient and was capable of landing on shorter runways. It could also handle extreme weather conditions and, as such, was ideal for reaching and operating from remote locations. The unusual layout of engines at the rear of the aircraft was designed to give passengers a quieter experience compared to other more conventional contemporary aircraft with engines mounted in the wings. The first prototype flew in 1962 and, by 1965, it began to enter service with the RAF. All the initial VC10s in RAF service were named after servicemen who had been awarded the Victoria Cross. The VC10s served with No 10 Squadron, which was heavily involved in the support of Operation *Corporate* throughout the conflict.

Vickers VC10 XV106 (pictured left and overleaf) was the first VC10 called into action during the Falklands War. On 3 April 1982, it was despatched from Brize Norton to pick up Rex Hunt, the British Governor of the Falkland Islands, and the resident Royal Marines who had been captured during the initial Argentine invasion. The prisoners had been flown to the Uruguayan capital, Montevideo, just hours earlier by the Argentine invaders. The act of returning prisoners of war back to their respective countries via a neutral nation was continued throughout the conflict by both sides. The governor and Marines were instantly returned to the UK on board XV106, arriving at RAF Brize Norton on the morning of 5 April, after a quick technical stop on Ascension Island on the way. The repatriated British marines all volunteered to return to the conflict immediately and were instrumental in the eventual retaking of the Islands. XV106 returned to Uruguay two weeks later to collect more deported prisoners, including 13 scientists from the British Antarctic Survey.

XV106 was named after Victoria Cross recipient Thomas Mottershead, who flew FE2s during World War One. XV106 served its whole career with the RAF and had the privilege of flying the Queen and Prince Phillip to Zambia for an official visit on 27 July 1979. In 1994, it was converted to a C1K variant, capable of carrying passengers and working as a tanker aircraft. Sadly, it was broken up in 2013, but the cockpit and a section of the fuselage were retained. The cockpit is now on display at the Avro Museum in Woodford, whereas the fuselage was given to the South Wales Aviation Museum.

In total, 13 VC10s of No 10 Squadron were operational in the South Atlantic during the conflict. In addition to flying personnel in and out in the air bridge role, they were also used as hospital transports, flying out the wounded from Ascension and Uruguay. A few of the aircraft were even given the famous Red Cross markings. After the attack on HMS *Sheffield*, the survivors were picked up by the tanker ship *British Esk* and taken to Wideawake, before being flown home to the UK on one of the VC10s. Even after the Argentine surrender, the VC10 fleet remained busy with yet more ambulance flights for several days. The VC10s were also tasked with returning Rex Hunt, newly made Civil Commissioner, to the Islands on 23 June 1982, to resume British rule of the Islands.

Vickers VC10 XR808 (pictured above inside and out) was delivered to the RAF in July 1966; it was named after Victoria Cross recipient Kenneth Campbell VC. It served much of its early career in and out of Hong Kong and was also involved in the withdrawal of British military staff from Malta in 1972. Crucially for the Falklands campaign and beyond, XR808 was used at Boscombe Down in feasibility trials for use of the type as a tanker. A handful of VC10s were used in this role during the war. In 1982, XR808 was one of the 13 aircraft of No 10 Squadron available for air bridge duties between Britain and the South Atlantic. After the war, XR808 operated as a VIP transport and carried passengers throughout the 1980s, including Prime Minister Margaret Thatcher on one occasion. It was converted to a tanker aircraft in 1995 and served in this role for over 15 years. It is now on display at the RAF Museum in Cosford.

Vickers VC10 ZD241 (pictured below) started life as a civilian passenger aircraft for British Overseas Airways Corporation (BOAC) in 1963. Its civilian registration was cancelled in April 1981 when it entered RAF service. Although it would have been available for use in the South Atlantic, it remained in storage for the RAF for over 10 years before being converted to a K4 tanker. ZD241 was not involved in the war, but it did serve in the Falklands for over 6 months, after being deployed there in September 2012. After retirement, ZD241 was delivered to Bruntingthorpe aerodrome, where it remained live and performed regular fast taxi runs. Sadly, the aerodrome was recently sold and, at the time of writing, the future of ZD241 is uncertain.

In 1959, the British military was committed to protecting the vast British Empire and set up a mounting base strategy, so that all areas of the Empire could be protected at short notice from

strategically placed outposts. In order to fulfil this, three new transport aircraft types were requested by the Ministry of Defence. They were looking for a strategic airlifter, strategic trooper and a tactical airlifter. The VC10 filled the role of the trooper, and the Hercules was eventually acquired for the role of tactical airlifter. The Short Belfast was chosen for the strategic airlift role and entered RAF service in 1966. However, the withdrawal from the British Empire happened a lot faster than anticipated and the need to protect distant colonies was taken off the list of priorities.

By 1975, the withdrawal from the Empire was largely complete and the aircraft required to support campaigns 'East of Suez' were considered superfluous and, therefore, quickly retired from the RAF. The Short Belfast fell victim to this new change of policy, and the example pictured below (XR371, *Enceladus*) was delivered directly to the RAF Museum at Cosford in 1976, where it remains today. Meanwhile, the

other Belfasts were sold to civilian companies, including five that were purchased by Transmeridian Air Cargo (TAC). Ironically, when Argentina invaded the Falklands, the need for these larger transports became apparent and the RAF leased them back from TAC for use during the war. The leased Belfasts proved vital during Operation *Corporate* for carrying larger equipment, including helicopters. Extra transport capacity was also provided by civilian Boeing 707s.

One additional transport type is also worthy of a brief footnote in the support of the campaign. After the unexpected invasion, the Hawker Siddeley Dominie T1 was an

important crew and pilot trainer at the time and many of the pilots involved in the conflict would have earned their wings on board the Dominie. It was the military version of the HS125 business jet and was used in the communication, liaison and VIP transport role for the RAF.

When the surprise invasion of the Falklands took place, the British military quickly scrambled all available assets to the area, but its senior commanders knew it would not be enough. In order to support the initial task force, additional shipping and aircraft would be required. Air Vice Marshall Ken Hayr was tasked with forming an additional Harrier squadron and sent his Dominie to collect pilots, such as Sqn Ldr Bob Iverson, who was tasked to inspect a container ship for potential use as a carrier. Without the Dominie to hand, Iverson would not have been able to make the journey from Peterborough to Liverpool in time. The Dominie (pictured above internally and below externally) is currently on display at the RAF Museum in Cosford and was used primarily as a trainer throughout its career.

By the end of the Falklands campaign, the RAF Hercules and VC10s had flown over 500 sorties to the South Atlantic, delivering over 5,000 people and 6,000 tons of freight. Additionally, the Hercules had key roles in airdropping men and cargo to the task force and onto the island itself during the actual invasion. Meanwhile, the VC10s worked hard on additional ambulance flights and, like a handful of Hercules aircraft, in the air-to-air refuelling trials. It is no over-estimation to say that the war could not have been won without the support of these aircraft and their crew. Operation *Corporate* was driven by logistics, ensuring enough personnel, equipment, fuel and firepower reached the remote South Atlantic Islands and was the first crucial step in retaking them.

Chapter 3

Bridging the Gap: Air-to-Air Refuelling Aircraft

Throughout the Falklands campaign, the major issue for the whole aerial operation was range. Air-to-air refuelling was key in extending the reach of both the RAF's and Fleet Air Arm's aircraft. At the time of the invasion, the Handley Page Victor K2 was the only strategic tanker in service with the RAF – it was clear that they would be playing a huge role in the retaking of the islands. In 1982, there were 23 Victors available, and all these aircraft would be required in one capacity or another during the conflict. Nos 55 and 57 squadrons were the primary operators of Victors at the time, but No 232 Operational Conversion Unit Squadron borrowed some of the Victors to fulfil the training roles from time to time. Victors would be essential in supporting operations in all aspects of the conflict, including refuelling transport aircraft along the air bridge, assisting aircraft in reaching the area and, most crucially, supporting aircraft in operations over the island, including the famous *Black Buck* bombing raids.

One of the first tasks given to the Victor fleet was currency training in air-to-air refuelling for pilots. Air-to-air refuelling was not common practice for many aircraft types in the RAF prior to the conflict. In some cases, like that of the Vulcan force, it was a forgotten skill only known to a handful of current pilots. For other types, like the C-130 Hercules, aircraft would need to be modified to receive fuel in flight. Either way, aircraft like Victor XL231 (pictured below) would be put to work in training and refreshing pilots and crew in the art of air-to-air refuelling. XL231 was one of the aircraft tasked with working up both Nimrod and Hercules crews prior to their departures to the South Atlantic. XL231 also flew out to Ascension in direct support of the RAF's No 1 (F) Squadron Harrier GR3s on 2 May 1982. After returning to the UK for more training duties, it returned to Wideawake alongside

the newly modified Hercules C1P aircraft on 14 June 1982, where it remained until the end of the month. XL231 continued operations between the UK and the Falklands until 1985. It is now on display at the Yorkshire Air Museum in its first Gulf War colours. It is one of the few Victors still capable of ground running its engines.

Most of the surviving Handley Page Victors were converted to K2 tankers in the late 1970s, though Victor XH648 is an exception. It was originally built in the late 1950s as a B1 model but, in 1965, after issues were spotted on the wing spars of the Vickers Valiant fleet, which were then fulfilling the tanking role, it became clear that a new tanking aircraft was required. As such, six B1 Victors, including XH648, were converted to two-point tankers, which could operate as bombers or tankers. These were designated B1A(K2P) aircraft, and all other suitable Victors were converted to dedicated tankers, known as the K2. XH648 was selected for preservation and retired to Duxford on 2 June 1976. It was kept outside for many years and, as such, was at the mercy of the elements. It is seen here shortly before undergoing a full restoration in 2016 (see above) and stripped back as it appeared in 2021 (see below). Once complete, it will be the only Victor on show that retains its bombing configuration.

Shortly after World War Two, the British government began the quest to develop its own nuclear bombing capability in order to keep pace with the rest of the world. Being able to deliver its own nuclear

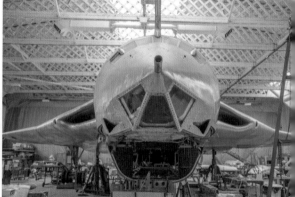

bomb seemed the best deterrent to any would-be attackers at this time. In the 1950s, Britain produced three strategic jet bombers, which became known as the V-bombers: the Vickers Valiant, Handley Page Victor and Avro Vulcan. Initially, these bombers were all designed for high altitude bombing, in the belief they would be safe from interception at height. However, after a US Lockheed U-2 spy craft was shot down at high altitude over the USSR in 1960, tactics were switched to low-level bombing attacks.

The move to low-altitude operations took its toll on the V-bombers. The Valiant was the most unsuitable and was converted from bombing into the tanking role in 1962. However, soon after this,

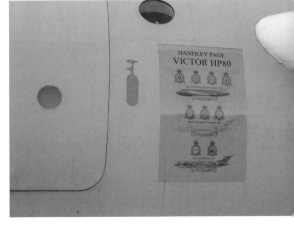

issues with its fatigue life were spotted and the airframe was retired completely. The Handley Page Victors were then selected for conversion into tankers to replace the Valiants from 1968 onwards. By 1982, the Avro Vulcan was the only remaining large bomber in British military service.

At the time of the Falklands War, all the Victor K2s wore a standard matt dark green and medium sea grey camouflage with white undersides. Most of these aircraft were given new markings after the war for later campaigns. Therefore, those preserved mostly appear in those colours today. Handley Page Victor XM715 wears its Operation *Granby* markings from the First Gulf War, but it also saw extensive service during the campaign to retake the Falklands.

It was flown by Flt Lt Frank Milligan to Ascension Island on 18 April 1982, in the first wave of Victors. Two days later, XM715 was put to work supporting maritime radar reconnaissance missions to South Georgia. XM715 returned to the UK via Dakar on 26 April to support the build-up and deployment of additional Harrier aircraft, including replacement Royal Navy Sea Harriers and RAF GR3 Harriers, which were taken to Ascension to protect the base.

During XM715's second stint in the South Atlantic, it supported further reconnaissance missions – this time refuelling Nimrods as part of Operation *Tuppence*. For *Tuppence 9*, XM715 was airborne for 7 hours and 40 minutes, whilst the Nimrod it refuelled remained in the air for a record breaking 19 hours. During its time in the South Atlantic, XM715 also supported the Hercules transports during Operation *Cadbury* on their airdrop flights, providing vital supplies to the frontline task force.

XM715 (pictured below) also flew during the *Black Buck* raids, providing air-to-air refuelling to the Avro Vulcan on its way to bomb strategic targets on the Islands. On 13 June 1982, XM715 returned to the UK in support of Vulcan XM597, which had been recovered from Rio de Janeiro after diverting there following a refuelling issue on *Black Buck 6*. Whilst in the UK, XM715 continued training sorties directly relating to the Falklands War, including air-to-air refuelling training for Nimrod and Hercules pilots. Even after the Argentine surrender, this Victor continued to visit the South Atlantic in support of Hercules transports for another two-and-a-half years.

In 1993, when the RAF retired its Victor tankers, XM715 was purchased by the Walton family and flown to Bruntingthorpe Aerodrome. It has been maintained in ground running condition, and up until recently, when the aerodrome changed hands, it has been demonstrated on regular Cold War Jet fast taxi days. In 2009, one of these fast taxi demonstrations resulted in an accidental take-off and

XM715 flew a short flight of around 100ft, which is widely recognised as the last flight of a Handley Page Victor.

The Handley Page Victor was the third of the V-bombers to enter service. It was designed by Godfrey Lee, based on an initial crescent-wing design by German scientist Dr Gustave Lachmann. It was designated the HP.80 and first flew in prototype form in December 1952. Development was not without its issues and, on 14 July 1954, the tailplane detached from one of the protypes during a routine test flight, killing all crew on board. Eventually the issues were

resolved, and the first Victors began to enter RAF service in the spring of 1958. It proved to be the most robust and adaptable of the V-bombers and, as such, was the last to retire, remaining in service until 15 October 1993.

During the Falklands War, it was constantly called upon to support operations via its primarily role (at the time) of air-to-air refuelling. Possibly the most remarkable achievement of the Victor tankers was their part in the now famous *Black Buck* raids. The mission was to get one Vulcan bomber (a second would take off on each mission as a spare) from Ascension to the Falkland Islands and back, so that it could drop its ordinance on specific strategic targets. In the first mission, the runway at Port Stanley was the target – a hit on this runway would prevent the Argentine Air Force from operating fast jets from the Island. In order to get the Vulcan to the target, a complex air-to-air refuelling plan was concocted, which would see 11 Victors and two Vulcans take to the skies on the night of 30 April 1982. A further seven Victors would take off in the early hours the following morning to help recover the Vulcans and Victors returning from the first wave.

Handley Page Victor XH672 (see next page) was heavily involved in Operation *Corporate* and through two flights on the night of 30 April/1 May flew almost 14 hours in total on the first *Black Buck* mission. Initially captained by Squadron Leader (Sqn Ldr) M D Todd on the first flight, and later by Sqn Ldr B R Neal, XH672 was also involved in *Black Buck* missions 2, 6 and 7. Additionally, XH672 also flew key missions supporting the FRS1 Sea Harriers aboard *Atlantic Conveyor* and was involved in supporting two GR3 Harriers that were deployed to HMS *Hermes* from Ascension on 1 June 1982. After three months of almost constant operations, XH672 was eventually flown back to RAF Marham via a short stop at Dakar on 15 June 1982. It is now on display at the RAF Museum in Cosford, in between the only complete Vickers Valiant and fellow *Black Buck* veteran, Vulcan XM598.

The extensive use of the ageing Victors for air-to-air refuelling did not go unnoticed and trails began to find alternate aircraft for the role. Although it was the only strategic tanker available at the start of the conflict, the RAF had already recognised the limited lifespan of the ageing Cold War bombers' airframes, even before the war began. In 1978, the RAF announced its intention to form a squadron of nine VC10 tankers by converting existing aircraft. The work was carried out at British Aerospace, Filton, in Bristol. The first of these aircraft did not make its first flight until 22 June 1982. This was a little too late to make an impact on the war itself, but they were put into use in the recovery programme following the conflict and remained part of the RAF presence in the Falklands for many years to come.

Following the Falklands conflict, the Vickers VC10 became one of the RAFs primary tanking aircraft. The trials proved so successful that the RAF purchased a further 14 Super VC10s from British Airways in 1981 to convert to tankers. Although they were in the hands of the RAF before the Argentine

invasion, they remained firmly in storage and were not used until their eventual conversion to K4 tankers in the 1990s. Many of these 14 aircraft were found to have extensive corrosion to the lower wing surfaces and required considerable work to get them up to specification. The VC10 remained in RAF service as a tanker until 2012, when it was retired. A few of these aircraft were saved for preservation, including VC10 K4 ZD241 (pictured above), which is now owned by GJD Services, based at Bruntingthorpe, Leicestershire. It was one of the 14 aircraft purchased from British Airways in 1981, formally carrying the serial G-ASGM.

The conversion of VC10 aircraft was not the only plan to relieve the pressure on the Handley Page Victor tankers. At the height of the conflict, on 1 May 1982, Lockheed Hercules C1 XV296 was delivered to Marshalls in Cambridge for reconfiguration trails as a tanker aircraft. After much modification and several test flights, an acceptable solution was found, and the first of six Hercules tanking aircraft entered service on 5 July 1982. Although too late for service in the war, the six aircraft were also used extensively in the South Atlantic in the recovery operation and the continued attempt to protect the Islands from future threats.

The RAF had one other large aircraft at its disposal – the Avro Vulcan, which was due to be retired imminently. Six of the remaining airframes (XH558, XH560, XH561, XJ825, XL445 and XM571) were selected for modification and the first, XH561, arrived at the Woodford works on 4 May 1982. The trials were successful, but the modifications were not completed until 18 June 1982. As the Argentine forces had surrendered four days earlier, the project was not rolled out more widely, and the phased rundown of the Vulcan force was continued.

Despite continued experimentation with existing aircraft, the aftermath of the Falklands War revealed a desperate need for the RAF to re-equip its tanker fleet. As such, it purchased nine L-1011-500s Lockheed Tristars from ex-airline stock. The initial order for six ex-British Airways aircraft was placed as early as December 1982, with the further three aircraft being acquired from Pan American in 1984. These nine aircraft proved vital in maintaining a continued presence in the South Atlantic, until they were eventually retired themselves in 2014. Six of these aircraft were placed in long-term storage at Bruntingthorpe Aerodrome for their new American owners, some of which have since been scrapped.

Above: The RAF Museum's Lockheed Hercules on a rainy evening at Cosford.

Left: Avro Vulcan B2 XH558, the last airworthy Vulcan, was not deployed south but was selected for conversion to a tanker aircraft just after the war.

Below: Former RAF Lockheed L-1011 Tristar, ZD950, in storage at Bruntingthorpe.

Chapter 4

Small Ship Helicopters: Rotary Aircraft Part One

I n total, 170 British helicopters were deployed to the South Atlantic, and they proved vital to the war effort in several roles including troop and cargo transport, anti-submarine, heavy-lifting and ground attack. The FAA, RAF and Army Air Corp (AAC) all operated their own helicopters throughout the campaign as part of the combined forces' task force. Recent downsizing and defence cuts coupled with the unexpected invasion meant that there was a shortfall of helicopters available for the operation. The practicalities of a remote long-distance war called for as many helicopters as possible leading to semi-retired aircraft types such as the Westland Wasp being brought back to the front line. This meant that a diverse range of helicopter types, ranging in size and capability, served during the conflict.

This chapter focuses on the roles played by the smaller aircraft, which included the Gazelles and Scouts of the AAC and the Wasps of the FAA. These small, versatile aircraft were ideal for operations from smaller ships and could carry out troop transport, reconnaissance and casualty evacuation. The diminutive aircraft were also key in the movement of key supplies between ships and land and were even used in light attack roles carrying out anti-tank, anti-submarine and anti-shipping raids throughout the conflict.

Westland Wasp XT787 in the Falklands War-era markings of HMS *Endurance* Flight.

Today, several Gazelles are operated on the civilian register, some of which are flown by the Gazelle Squadron (pictured above) at UK airshows. The performance usually consists of a pair of Gazelles performing an aerial ballet in tribute to the Gazelle, Britain's longest serving military helicopter.

The AAC and 3 CBAS also used the Westland Scout AH1 alongside their Gazelles during the conflict. The Scout had been developed from the SARO P531 as a land-based Army support helicopter capable of carrying up to six personnel. Like the Gazelle, it was not designed or modified for use at sea but seemed to experience no major difficulties with flight operations from aircraft carriers and small ships during the war. Four of the Scout helicopters on board the frontline task force did, however, show some signs of corrosion from the saltwater and were stored below deck on *Elk*, one of the Merchant Navy support vessels, to prevent further damage.

One of these Scouts later became the victim of the only Argentine air-to-air victory of the war. On 28 May 1982, two Scouts of 3 CBAS were being positioned north of Goose Green in support of planned ground operations, and they were tasked with forwarding ammunition to the front line and returning

with casualties. They had already been flying for three hours when two Argentine FMA IA 58 Pucarás attacked the two helicopters. Despite evading several attacks, XT629 was eventually shot down by canon and rocket fire, killing Lt Richard Nunn, the pilot, instantly. The co-pilot, Sgt Bill Belcher, was thrown clear in the crash but left severely injured. He was later recovered by the other Scout helicopter flown by Captain (Capt) Jeff Niblett, who received the Distinguished Flying Cross (DFC) for his rescue efforts and continued support of the operations after the incident. Lt Nunn was also posthumously awarded the DFC for his actions. The support of the small helicopters from 3 CBAS is widely cited as instrumental in the eventual success of this operation.

Westland Scout AH1 XW612 (pictured above) was delivered to the AAC in 1970 and served for almost 30 years before being placed on the civil register. It was not directly part of the Falklands War effort but is a good representation of the aircraft serving there at the time. It is currently registered to Military Vehicle Solutions Ltd but has been seen regularly around UK airshows and events for several years. It is also available to hire for flight experiences via Dragonfly Aviation.

The first Westland Scout took to the skies on 29 August 1960 and quickly became the backbone of the Army's helicopter force. Although primarily a support, liaison and light transport aircraft, the Scout could also be fitted with a range of weapons and fulfilled light ground attack and anti-tank roles. It was also used for training and search and rescue duties. It could carry six people or be kitted out to fit a stretcher for the CASEVAC (casualty evacuation) role. When operating as a light attack helicopter, it could either carry two skid-mounted machine gun packs or a single machine gun in the rear cabin. It could also carry four SS11 anti-tank missiles, which were used to great effect during the Falklands War.

On 8 June 1982, Westland Scout XR628 suffered a rotor gearbox failure whilst taking cover from a pair of passing Argentine A-4 Skyhawks. XR628 was in a low hover over MacPhee Pond, once the Skyhawks had passed, the pilot began to climb but the gearbox failed, and he was forced to make an emergency landing. No one was hurt and the crew were recovered by another Scout helicopter. XR628 was written off and later recovered by a Sea King HC4 (Helicopter Commando Mark 4) and eventually returned to the UK. Tragically, the passing Skyhawks continued their flight to attack the Royal Fleet Auxiliary (RFA) support ships *Sir Galahad* and *Tristram*. Five RFA crewmen and 55 Welsh Guards were killed in the attack that also destroyed *Sir Galahad*, which remained on fire for over a week. This was the greatest loss of British life throughout the whole campaign; it became known as the 'tragedy at Bluff Cove'.

On 14 June 1982, the Scots Guards were approaching Mount Tumbledown when they were suddenly fired upon by an Argentine Howitzer battery. As the guns were out of range, the ground forces called in No 656 Squadron of the AAC for an aerial strike. Capt J G Greenhalgh was in the area, but his Scout was not equipped with the missiles, so he returned to base to be re-fitted. He returned 20 minutes later and surveyed the area. He was able to guide in another two Scout helicopters. The three Scouts then fired a succession of ten missiles, nine of which scored direct hits on the Argentine post, hitting the Howitzers, nearby bunkers, and an ammunition dump.

Westland Scout AH1 XT626 (pictured below) represents and commemorates the operations of British Army aviation as part of the high-profile Historic Army Aircraft Flight (HAAF). The HAAF displays its impressive collection of historic army aircraft regularly at airshows and events. XT626 served with the Territorial Army at Netheravon for most of its career, which began in 1963 and ended in 1994, when XT626 joined the HAAF. The aircraft is registered to the Historic Aircraft Flight Trust as G-CIBW.

The Westland Wasp was the 'twin' to the Scout. The development of the two helicopters began in 1957 at Saunders-Roe Ltd, with their initial design based on the successful SARO Skeeter. It began as a private venture, which was continued by Westland Helicopters when it took control of SARO in 1959, by which point it had completed two prototypes. The Wasp was designed as the Naval anti-submarine variant of the helicopter and featured a distinctive four-wheeled, spindly undercarriage.

The Wasp also sports some additional features that distinguish it from its Scout brother. Unique for its naval service, the main rotor blades and tail section can be folded in order to create space for stowage on a ship. The Wasp could be fitted with a range of weaponry, including two homing torpedoes

SARO Skeeter at the Solent Sky Museum – the Wasp and Scout designs were based on this helicopter; some features were retained.

or several depth charges or bombs. It was powered by a single 710hp Bristol (later Rolls Royce) Nimbus 503 turboshaft engine. The first Wasp HAS1s entered service with the FAA in October 1963, and a total of 98 eventually saw Royal Navy service. At the time of the Falklands War, the Wasps were on the verge of retirement, slowly being phased out in favour of the new Lynx HAS2.

Westland Wasp HAS1 G-BYCX (see right and below) did not serve with the Royal Navy but was instead one of the many exported to serve abroad. The Brazilian, South African, New Zealand and Netherlands naval air

forces all purchased them. G-BYCX served with the South African Air Force and spent some time in New Zealand, where it was restored to ground running condition. It was eventually shipped to the UK and registered as G-BYCX and is now available to hire for flight experiences via Dragonfly Aviation.

In 1982, No 829 Naval Air Squadron still had a good number of Wasps serving under the command of Lieutenant Commander (Lt Cdr) M J Mullane. Most of the small and medium-sized ships in the Royal Navy had their own 'Flight', which consisted of a single helicopter and its crew. The Wasps were based out of Royal Naval Air Station (RNAS) Portland (HMS *Osprey*) but at the time of the invasion they were spread far and wide on board several different vessels, including the ice patrol ship HMS *Endurance*. *Endurance* was to become one of the most well-known ships of the conflict; the ship was docked at Port Stanley when, on 19 March 1982, a group of what was thought to be Argentine scrap metal dealers raised the Argentine flag on South Georgia. *Endurance* was despatched to deploy the small band of Marines on the island to ward off the Argentines.

Although the initial action was unsuccessful, HMS *Endurance* joined the main task force and was able to assist in the successful retaking of South Georgia on 22 April 1982, by landing Special Boat Service (SBS) soldiers at Hound Bay. The task force moved to deeper waters and the two Wasps of *Endurance* were involved in the attack on the submarine *Santa Fe*, both of which fired AS12 anti-ship missiles and scored direct hits. HMS *Endurance* remained in the waters to keep the British flag waving and to continue to monitor the waters for enemy submarine activity.

Westland Wasp XT787 (pictured left) was built at the Fairey section of Westland Helicopters in 1967; it made its first flight on 19 January that year. XT787 operated on HMS *Leander* and HMS *Rhyl* and was spared retirement when the Falklands were invaded. Although XT787 was never actually deployed to the South Atlantic, it is currently painted in the South Atlantic camouflage scheme of HMS *Endurance*'s Wasp XS527, which took part in the attack of the *Santa Fe*. The scheme was hastily applied at the time after the distinctive bright red markings proved easy to spot (see page 42). XT787 is currently owned by Terry Martin, a former RAF wing commander who formed the Westland Wasp Historic Flight and displays the aircraft regularly.

Although the Wasp was primarily conceived as an anti-submarine helicopter, it was not always used in this role. The newer, more capable Lynx helicopter had largely replaced it at the time and, therefore, the Wasp was utilised in other supporting roles. The Lynx was a little too big to operate on the smaller British frigates. Three of the Royal Navy's survey ships, *Hecla*, *Hydra* and *Herald*, were converted to ambulance ships and given a helicopter Flight of Wasps each. The aircrew were quickly trained in nursing procedures and flew several practice flights during the passage to the South Atlantic.

Wasp HAS1 XT420 (G-CBUI, see below) is now operated by the Navy Wings charity, which is the civilian organisation born from the Royal Navy's official historic flight. XT420 made its first flight on 3 December 1964 and served with No 829 Naval Air Squadron on several different vessels. In 1982, it went to the South Atlantic on the converted survey ship HMS *Hecla*, which was one of the few ambulance ships in the fleet to be painted white with Red Cross markings. XT420 also received the Red Cross markings on its nose but otherwise retained the standard blue/grey markings.

XT420 joined the fleet on 20 April 1982, and stayed with *Hecla* throughout the conflict, eventually returning to the UK on 29 July 1982. It was involved in several ferrying flights of casualties but, on rotation out of the war zone on 29 May 1982, was forced to donate parts to the incoming Wasp on HMS *Herald*. XT420 was returned to serviceability at Montevideo on 2 June and returned to the action a few days later. It was retired in 1988 and disposed of by the Navy in 1994, eventually joining the

heritage flight. It has recently been repainted in its original HMS *Aurora* scheme that it wore in 1976, but it is seen here as it appeared in 2019.

As well as the ambulance ships and ice patrol vessels, three other frigates were deployed to the South Atlantic equipped with Wasp helicopters. These were HMS *Active*, *Plymouth* and *Yarmouth*. Midway through the conflict, three additional Flights were formed to equip the Merchant vessels deployed to support the main fleet. The Wasp (XT429) on board *Plymouth* also joined the attack on the unfortunate Argentine submarine *Santa Fe*, firing an AS12 missile that appeared to hit but caused no apparent damage. The Wasp continued its flight to assist the successful retaking of South Georgia. On 8 June, HMS *Plymouth* was hit by two bombs dropped by the Argentine Daggers of Grupo 6, and despite a 6ft hole in the ship, the vessel was able to limp to safety and receive repairs. XT429 received only minor splinter damage and was easily returned to operations.

Although overshadowed by other helicopter types, the Westland Wasps involved in Operation *Corporate* flew a total of 451 hours in 727 sorties, making an impressive 3,333 deck landings in the process. Wasp XS567 (see below) was deployed to the South Atlantic four days after the Argentine surrender as part of Apollo Flight. Most of the Royal Navy frigates and smaller ships were given a 'Flight', which usually consisted of a single helicopter and its crew. Each Flight was named after the ship it was on board. XS567 was deployed on board the Leander-class frigate, HMS *Apollo*. It remained with the ship and assisted in the aftermath of the war until October 1982, when it returned to the UK. It joined HMS *Endurance* in 1984 and remains preserved at IWM Duxford in these markings.

Chapter 5

Junglies and Pingers: Rotary Aircraft Part Two

Helicopters had a huge role to play in the Falklands War, and although they fulfilled many duties, the majority of the time they were either performing transport or anti-submarine tasks. In the Royal Navy, the transport aircraft operated by the Commando squadrons were known as Junglies. They were primarily tasked with troop transport, but were also capable of moving supplies and ammunition if required. During the Falklands War, the Westland Sea King HC4 and the Westland Wessex HU5 (Helicopter Utility Mark 5) were the main Junglies.

The Royal Navy also deployed helicopters in the anti-submarine role – these became known as Pingers. The Westland Lynx HAS2 (Helicopter Anti-Submarine), Westland Sea King HAS2 and HAS5 and Westland Wessex HAS3 were the primary Pingers during the war. The Pingers were equipped with radar and underwater sonar and could also carry anti-submarine torpedoes and depth charges. They maintained 24-hour surveillance in the war zone, constantly looking out for submarines. The Sea Kings were based on the larger aircraft carriers such as HMS *Hermes* and *Invincible*, whilst the smaller

Westland Sea King HC4 ZF122 has recently been returned to the skies by Historic Helicopters. It is a more recent variant, and there are very few left flying in the UK today.

Old vs new in a flypast at Yeovilton Air Day in 2019; a Wessex and two Wasps lead the Royal Navy's modern Merlin and Wildcat helicopters.

Wessex helicopters equipped the County-class destroyers HMS *Antrim* and *Glamorgan*. A handful of the HAS2 Sea Kings were stripped of their sonars and converted to troop transport Junglies.

Although not a Junglie in the Royal Navy, the RAF Chinook helicopter performed a similar role during the conflict and its huge carrying capacity made it an indispensable asset during the war. The Boeing Chinook is an American-built helicopter with a unique tandem rotor lay out. It was first conceived in 1957 and its impressive performance and heavy-lift capability have made it one of the most adaptable and versatile helicopters ever produced. It has been exported all over the world and at the time of the Falklands War, it was in use by both the British and Argentine forces.

In April 1982, five RAF Chinook HC1s from No 18 Squadron were loaded aboard the modified container ship MV *Atlantic Conveyor*. One was left on Ascension Island to assist operations there, whilst *Atlantic Conveyor* sailed further south to join the main task force. ZA707 remained behind and in a three-week period flew over 100 hours with no major serviceability issues – lifting an incredible 350 tonnes of equipment in a single day.

On 25 May 1982, Chinook ZA718, known after its code as *Bravo November* (pictured below) was sent to pick up cargo from HMS *Glasgow* when *Atlantic Conveyor* was attacked by an Argentine Dassault Super Étendard. An Exocet missile scored a direct hit causing a fire to break out, the rapid spread of which prevented the evacuation of any of the other aircraft on board. Three of the vital Chinooks were lost that day, but *Bravo November* was airborne and safely landed on HMS *Hermes*. Significantly, the Chinook tools, lubricants and spares were also lost with *Atlantic Conveyor,* but *Bravo November* was able to continue operations, with its workload quadrupled without these essentials for several weeks. It was the only heavy lift helicopter available to the task force for some time.

Bravo November was delivered to the RAF as an HC1 (Helicopter-Cargo) variant in February 1982. By 29 March of that year, it had joined No 18 Squadron at RAF Odiham where it received its famous 'BN' code. On 25 April, it set sail for the South Atlantic with the other four Chinooks. After the other Chinooks were lost, *Bravo November* continued to push forward with the ground forces as they broke through the Argentine defences. On 30 May, ZA718 was on a mission flown by Sqn Ldr Dick Langworthy and his co-pilot Flt Lt Andy Lawless to deliver weapons to SAS troops, who were under attack from heavy artillery fire. Under the cover of darkness, despite help from night-vision googles, the crew struggled to find a suitable place to deliver the cargo on the uneven ground. Eventually, they delicately landed on boggy ground in the middle of an active firing area where they managed to avoid sinking and dropped off the weapons only to run into a snowstorm on the way back. The night-vision equipment began to fail, and the altimeter had developed a fault. Inevitably, *Bravo November* impacted the water as it returned towards *Hermes*. Despite the engines ingesting water, the radio antenna being lost, the cockpit door ripped off and holes in the fuselage, ZA718 was able to limp home. Sqn Ldr Langworthy earned a DFC for his efforts.

On 2 June 1982, ZA718 carried two loads of fully armed paratroopers, totalling 156 personnel, to an advanced position just 10 miles outside of Port Stanley. The unstoppable Chinook continued to support the paratroopers by dropping ammunition and supplies and evacuating the injured. It was

Chinook ZA718 *Bravo November* currently on display at the RAF Museum, Cosford, next to fellow Falklands War veteran Harrier GR3 XZ997.

Re-enactors Jed Jaggard and Adam Cockerill recreate a period scene with Chinook ZA718 *Bravo November* at the RAF Museum.

even required to recover two damaged Sea King helicopters. By the end of the war, *Bravo November* had carried around 1,500 troops, 95 casualties, 650 prisoners and 550 tons of cargo.

ZA718 (pictured below) served with the RAF until 2022, undergoing several upgrades and taking part in almost every major conflict since the Falklands, earning its nickname 'The Survivor'. Over the course of its service, it helped four pilots earn their DFCs. The RAF continues to operate a large fleet of upgraded Boeing Chinooks with vastly improved technologies on board. ZA718 has recently been rewarded with retirement and is now on display at the RAF Museum, Cosford.

The versatile Westland Wessex served with the Royal Navy and the RAF for over 44 years, serving in a diverse range of roles from VIP transport and training to anti-submarine and troop transport. The Wessex also saw action in Borneo, Northern Ireland and, of course, the Falklands. Several variants of the Wessex were produced, each adapted to their specific roles. The HAS1 served well in the utility capacity for the FAA but was not a purpose-built troop transport. The RAF's HC2, which could carry up to 16 troops, led the way for the development of the HU5, which had an improved load-lifting capacity and an excellent safety margin due to its twin Gnome engines – making it the ideal choice for Royal Navy operations in the South Atlantic in 1982. The HU5 also became the most capable search and rescue Wessex, its new engines doubled the power of the helicopter and had an extra 90 miles of range over previous variants. This gave a crucial life or death advantage when searching for lost casualties at sea. The extra power also enabled the helicopter to operate in more challenging conditions, like those faced in the South Atlantic.

The Wessex crews of A Flight experienced a tough opening to their war when, on 30 April, Wessex HU5 XS483 was detached to HMS *Glamorgan* to support the Lynx anti-submarine flights from HMS *Alacrity* on that day. The Wessex was fired upon by two Tigercat missiles but somehow escaped unscathed. Less than a week later the Flight was sent to assist the search for survivors after the sinking of HMS *Sheffield*. For the next few weeks, the Wessex helicopters of A Flight were busy engaging in VERTREP (vertical replenishment) and transfer sorties but, on 11 June 1982, they were given one of the most unusual missions of the war.

An SBS patrol had discovered that the Argentine commanders, including General de Brigada Menendez, held a meeting each morning in the Port Stanley Town Hall. The SBS concluded that a final blow to the enemy's military commanders would surely bring a swift end to the conflict. A secret

Westland Sea King HAR3 XZ585 on display at the RAF Museum in Hendon – showing the famous yellow RAF scheme – this aircraft remained in Europe, serving for the RAF in the search and rescue role, at the time of the war.

The Westland Sea King was a British-built helicopter, based upon the American Sikorsky S61 design. The Westland version is heavily modified for British purposes, using a full suite of British anti-submarine systems and Rolls-Royce Gnome engines, instead of the General Electric T58s used in the American original. The Sea King was first designed to replace the Wessex in the

Westland Sea King XV661 HU5SAR showing the Royal Navy's last search and rescue colour scheme. This aircraft did deploy to the Falklands just after the Argentine surrender in its HAS5 configuration.

anti-submarine role, but like its predecessor, its role soon expanded, and the Sea King soon operated as a commando-carrying Junglie, as well as an anti-submarine Pinger. The Sea King was also used by both the RAF and Royal Navy in the search and rescue role, appearing in the famous bright yellow of the RAF or red and grey for the Navy. As well as the Falklands campaign, the Sea King also served in the Gulf, Bosnian, Iraq and Afghanistan wars before being retired completely from British service by 2018.

During the Falklands War, a few variants of Sea Kings were deployed, including the HC4, as the primary Junglies, supported by ten HAS2 Sea Kings that had been stripped of their sonar equipment. The anti-submarine role was carried out by HAS2 and HAS5 Sea Kings, most of these were based on the larger Royal Navy ships, such as the HMS *Hermes* and *Invincible*.

Except for the Boeing Chinook (of which only a limited number were available for British forces), the Sea King was the largest and most capable helicopter in the South Atlantic. In its HC4 configuration,

it could carry up to 28 fully equipped commandoes. It had an impressive range of around 600 miles without refuelling and, being a recent arrival into the forces, it was equipped with the most modern equipment for navigation and communication. The Sea King, like most of the helicopters discussed in this chapter, was also versatile and could be modified to suit a range of tasks. As the HC4, it was Britain's first choice for ferrying troops and equipment to the front line.

Sea King HC4 ZA298 (pictured right and below) is known as the *King of the Junglies*. It clocked up over 34 years of service with the FAA, serving in conflicts from the

Falklands to Afghanistan, receiving battle damage in both wars. ZA298 was even chosen to carry the Olympic Flame for the London 2012 Olympics where it famously lowered a Royal Marine into the Tower of London. It survived a rocket-propelled grenade attack in Afghanistan in 2011 and was also hit by small arms fire during the Gulf wars. It has recently been retired to the Fleet Air Arm Museum at RNAS Yeovilton, where it currently appears alongside an impressive collection of Falklands aircraft.

On 3 April 1982, ZA298 embarked on HMS *Hermes* where it sailed to Ascension Island. For the first couple of weeks after arrival, *King of the Junglies* was left at Wideawake Airfield to carry out helicopter delivery and vertical replenishment tasks. On 8 May, it joined HMS *Fearless* en route to the total exclusion zone, taking up position in San Carlos Water. On 25 May, Lt Cdr Simon Thornewell flew ZA298 on a rescue mission to HMS *Coventry*, which had been attacked by Argentine Air Force A-4 Skyhawks and left stricken. Aircrewman Chief Petty Officer M J Tupper was credited with saving over 40 lives that day.

On 13 June 1982, Lt Cdr Thornewell was once again at the helm when ZA298 was attacked by an Argentine Skyhawk A-4b flown by Alferez Dellapiane. The Skyhawk fired its canons at the Sea King. One of the shells went through the main rotor blade just before it exploded. Somehow, the cool-headed Thornewell was able to land safely in Impassable Valley without any injuries to himself or the crew. Within two hours, another Sea King (ZA291) arrived with a new rotor blade, the repairs were made and, less than two hours after that, *King of the Junglies* was back in the air again.

On 15 June 1982, ZA298 was given the final task of the war when Thornewell and his crew were tasked with ferrying General de Brigada Menendez and four of his most senior officers out of Port Stanley and onto HMS *Fearless*, signifying the end of Argentine occupation of the Falklands.

The Sea King was first conceived as a helicopter specialising in the anti-submarine role, by the time of the Falklands War, the third version of the anti-submarine warfare variant was well into production. This was the HAS5 with MEL Super Searcher Radar encased in a large dorsal radome (clearly visible in this image below of XZ574). It was also equipped with a new, state-of-the-art acoustic processing system that could be used with sonobuoys. Sonobuoys were an expendable system of devices that could be dropped into the sea from the air to detect underwater sound using hydrophones. The data could then be pinged back to the helicopter in order to detect signs and signals from enemy submarines.

Sea King HAS5 XZ574 (see previous page) belonged to No 820 NAS in 1982 and sailed on board HMS *Invincible* on 5 April 1982. On 23 April, shortly after reaching the total exclusion zone, XZ574 was called into action to search for another Sea King, which had been forced to ditch in the sea. XZ574 was crewed by Sub Lieutenant C P Heweth, Prince Andrew, Lt McAlister and Leading Aircrewman Arnull, who managed to locate the stricken Sea King and pilot but were unable to find crewman Petty Officer Casey, who became the first British casualty of the war.

On 2 June, XZ574 was once again called upon to locate and rescue a British pilot. This time, Lt Cdr Dudley and his crew were on the lookout for Flt Lt Mortimer, who had spent eight hours in the water after ejecting from his No 801 Squadron Sea Harrier, which had been shot down by a Roland missile.

Above: Falklands veteran Westland Sea King XV659 is now used at RAF Cosford for engineer training.

Right: Internal shots of Sea King XV659. It was an HAS2A during the Falklands War but was later converted to an HAS6 variant.

ZA128 is another of RAF Cosford's engineering Sea Kings that took part in the conflict as an HAS5; it too was later converted to HAS6 specification.

The rescue mission was a success and Mortimer was picked up relatively unharmed. XZ574 remained in the South Atlantic until 28 August when it returned to Britain with HMS *Invincible*. XZ574 is now at the Fleet Air Arm Museum but is not currently on public display. It is seen here making an appearance at Yeovilton Air Day in 2019.

In addition to the new HAS5 anti-submarine Sea Kings, the Royal Navy also deployed several slightly older HAS2s. Although these were slightly outdated, the full roll-out of the new model was not complete when Argentina invaded the Falklands. Some of the HAS2s supported the updated HAS5s in the patrol for enemy ships and submarines, which was maintained with a Sea king airborne 24 hours a day. Other HAS2s were stripped of their electronics and used as additional Junglies, ferrying troops and cargo. By the end of the conflict, the Sea Kings of No 824 NAS alone had delivered 2,000 tonnes of stores between ships, in a total of 650 operating hours.

Pressure on the Royal Navy's Sea Kings was immense and the operations at Wideawake Airfield were adversely affected by the departure of some of its helicopters to support the main task force and replace lost or unserviceable helicopters. As all the Royal Navy helicopters were occupied, the RAF were asked to spare one of its search and rescue helicopters from No 202 Squadron, along with an additional Chinook. Sea King HAR3 XZ593 was selected for deployment and was packed into a Short Belfast and arrived on Ascension on 8 May 1982. It was immediately put to work on vertical replenishment, search and rescue and logistical support.

Sea King HAR3 XV659 (pictured on previous page) also served with No 202 Squadron, but was not chosen for deployment to the Falklands, though it does illustrate the type well. It entered service in 1978 and spent its whole career as a search and rescue unit and was actively saving lives around UK waters during the time of the Falklands. It is now enjoying semi-retirement at RAF Cosford where it is used for ground instruction in the School of Engineering based there.

The Sea King was noted for its high levels of reliability and, during the conflict, it was almost taken for granted that a Sea King would be serviceable. The only real issue was the erosion of the rotor

blades due to the extreme weather conditions experienced. That said, almost 50 modifications were incorporated to the Sea King design during the conflict, and it was the first test of this relativity new helicopter, which would go on to serve with distinction throughout its career.

The Westland Lynx can lay claim to being the last mass-produced all-British designed helicopter. It served with the British armed forces for over 40 years. It was designed as a small, agile multi-role helicopter that proved so successful that it saw service in almost every major operational theatre, including providing humanitarian assistance, geological surveys, counterterrorism and war. It has also served all over the world and proved equally as reliable in the heat of the Caribbean or the cold of the Antarctic. The Lynx also held the record as the fastest helicopter anywhere in the world for 46 years after XX153 (now preserved at the Army Flying Museum) achieved a speed of 200mph.

Although the origins of the Lynx can be traced back to the early 1960s, it did not enter military service until 1976 when No 700L NAS took delivery of the first batch and formed the Intensive Flying Trials Unit (IFTU). The first operational Lynx helicopters belonged to the AAC when the AH1 entered service in 1979. The FAA adopted the Lynx HAS2 two years later. They also served for 3 CBAS of the Royal Marines and the Commando Helicopter Force (CHF) and were exported to a dozen different nations as well.

During the Falklands War, the Royal Navy operated the Lynx HAS2 Anti-Submarine Warfare (ASW) alongside its fleet of anti-submarine Sea Kings, to help maintain the 24-hour patrol around the task force. No 815 NAS took the Lynx HAS2 into battle, deploying a helicopter to 23 different ships. As they were new to service, they had not yet reached full capacity and the Wasps of No 829 NAS, which were due to be replaced, had to wait a little longer for retirement. The diminutive Lynx was ideal for operations on the frigates and destroyers at the time of the conflict. The Lynx was painted in an Oxford blue colour scheme that was eventually replaced with the grey scheme, but not until after the war was over.

Westland Lynx HAS2 XZ721, known as *Gonzo*, was flown to Ascension Island on board a C-130 Hercules on 9 April 1982. It was one of the few helicopters to be fitted with the Sea Skua missiles at that time and so was in great demand. *Gonzo* was transferred to HMS *Brilliant,* but not for long. When *Brilliant* was attached to Operation *Paraquat*, the mission to retake South Georgia, XZ721 was transferred to HMS *Sheffield*. Fortunately, *Gonzo*, was unscathed and able to escape when the two Argentine Super Étendards attacked and sank *Sheffield*. The Lynx safely landed on board HMS *Hermes* before rejoining HMS *Brilliant* on 7 May 1982. XV721's biggest success was being involved in harassing the requisitioned Argentine coastal freighter *Monsunen* to such a point that it caused it to run aground on 23 May 1982. *Gonzo* is now based at the East Midlands Aeropark.

Falklands veteran Westland Lynx HAS2 XZ721 awaiting some restoration work underneath the Avro Vulcan B2A XM575 at the East Midlands Aeropark.

The Lynx was one of the first helicopters to be equipped with the Sea Skua missile and, on route to the Falklands, it was decided that the Lynx would operate as a gunship too. Therefore, experiments took place on HMS *Brilliant* to fit a machine gun rigging to the deployed helicopters. On 3 May 1982, the first combat-firing of a Sea Skua missile took place when Lynx HAS2 XZ242 skimmed two missiles towards the Argentine patrol boat ARA *Alférez Sobral*. The damaged vessel was able to return to port for repairs, but eight personnel were killed, and the patrol boat was effectively taken out of the conflict.

Westland Lynx HAS2 XZ720, known as *Phoenix* (pictured opposite), first flew in April 1980 before joining No 815 NAS HMS *Heron* in November 1981. On 5 April 1982, *Phoenix* was on board the frigate HMS *Alacrity* when it set sail for the South Atlantic. During a brief stop on Ascension Island between the 16 and 18 April, XZ720 was used for training and submarine spotting patrols. As it was not fitted with Sea Skua missiles, it was transferred to HMS *Invincible* before it reached the Falkland Islands. *Phoenix* then spent the next few weeks swapping between RFA *Fort Austin*, HMS *Hermes* and HMS *Invincible* undertaking Electronic Surveillance Measures (ESM) missions and Exocet Missile decoy tasks.

XZ720 returned to the UK on 21 July 1982 and went on to have a distinguished career, serving in Operation *Granby*, the First Gulf war, this time fitted with Sea Skua missiles, which it used to great effect. After being retired in 2009, it was restored to its Gulf War paint scheme by the Lynx Project Team and gifted to the Fleet Air Arm Museum in 2012. It remains there on display today.

Westland Lynx XZ233 (pictured on the next page) was initially built as a HAS2 variant. It took its first flight in January 1977 and was deployed to the Falklands aboard HMS *Argonaut*, where it got the nickname 'Jason of the Argonaut'. XZ233 was very much involved in the thick of the action during the Falklands War. It took part in the rescue mission after HMS *Antelope* had been bombed by Argentine Skyhawks on 24 May 1982. XZ233 also attempted to engage the Argentine Navy with an air-to-surface Sea Skua missile but was unable to fire due to an electronics fault.

On 21 May 1982, the day the British ground forces landed, XZ233 was given the unenviable mission of acting as a decoy on behalf of the Royal Navy ships. The Lynx was tasked with hovering at 400ft with a 1m square metal box bolted to the side of the helicopter. The box was designed to draw any stray Exocet missiles away from the fleet. In the first action of the day, an Argentine Aermacchi 339 took off from Stanley airfield and rushed in to attack the hovering Lynx. However, it diverted at the last minute when it saw HMS *Argonaut* as a more tempting target.

Later in the war, XZ233 miraculously escaped an encounter with two Argentine Daggers, which tried and failed to shoot the Lynx down. On 13 June, Lt Chris Clayton was piloting XZ233 on a routine patrol when the two Daggers spotted the lynx, dropped their external fuel tanks and prepared to engage. Clayton's superb, evasive flying was enough to manoeuvre the agile Lynx out of the way of the oncoming fast jets, which eventually gave up and headed for home. Clayton was awarded a Mention in Dispatches for his skilful flying. He would go on to become a senior naval officer, eventually retiring as a rear admiral.

After the initial Argentine surrender on 14 June 1982, Lt Clayton was tasked with flying the commanding officer of 40 Commando, Lieutenant Colonel (Lt Col) Malcolm Hunt, to Port Howard to officially receive the surrender of the garrison based there. XZ233 would go on to serve the Royal Navy until the type's retirement in 2017. Two years later, it was passed on to Jet Art Aviation Ltd, which restored the aircraft. It now wears the Oxford Blue scheme, which would have been worn when it first entered service in the late 1970s. It is currently on display at the Yorkshire Air Museum.

The diverse collection of over 170 helicopters proved vital to the success of Operation *Corporate*, waging a war on such a remote set of Islands so far from a fixed British military base could not have been done without the flexibility provided by the helicopter force and their crews.

Chapter 6

Insight and Intel: Reconnaissance and Airborne Early Warning Aircraft

Airborne Early Warning (AEW) was a system used since the end of World War Two, where aircraft could patrol an area and use radar technology to locate any potential enemy aircraft threats long before they would be in range to attack. Although radar is considered a British invention, it was an American development towards the end of World War Two that led to its practical use in the early warning role. From 1949, the Douglas AD-3W Skyraider could be equipped with a Hughes AN/APS-20 radar that could pick up ships and formations of aircraft around 100 miles away. Impressed by America's use of the Skyraider during the Korean War, the Royal Navy ordered 50 of their own.

When the Skyraider was retired, the Fairey Gannet was chosen to replace it in the AEW role, but the Royal Navy would recycle and refit the AN/APS-20 radar systems and bolt them onto the Gannet. By 1978, only a handful of Gannet AEW3s were left in service and the retirement of larger aircraft carriers

Fairey Gannet at the Fleet Air Arm Museum.

The Shackleton Aviation Group's Avro Shackleton WR963 performing an evening engine run at Coventry Airport. Ambitious plans hope to return this aircraft to the air one day.

like HMS *Ark Royal* meant that they were no longer a viable option. The hand-me-down radar systems were passed on to the RAF, which fitted them to its Avro Shackletons and, although their 15 hours of endurance enabled excellent coverage of the UK airspace, the lack of air-to-air refuelling capability left them stranded in Britain and of no use to the task force in the South Atlantic.

In the middle of the 1970s, a proposal to replace the Shackletons in this role was put forward. The Shackleton itself was a development of the Avro Lancaster and was still using World War Two technology in many ways. The Hawker Siddeley Nimrod was suggested as a replacement, but the programme was plagued with issues and, by 1982, there was no sign of an AEW Nimrod. In fact, in 1986, the project was cancelled and the Shackletons continued in the role until the 1990s, when they were eventually replaced by Boeing E-3 Sentry aircraft. This left the Operation *Corporate* task force without an AEW capability.

Therefore, a shipborne aircraft would be needed to fulfil this role and the Westland Sea King was selected to fill it. The project to create an AEW Sea King was already under way in 1982, but when Argentina invaded the Falklands, the project was hurried along. After the project was given the full go-ahead, it took just 11 weeks to see the first aircraft in the theatre.

Initially, two Sea King HAS2s (XV650 and XV704) were equipped with the Searchwater radar attached to the underside of the helicopter on a swivel arm encased in a protective, inflatable dome.

This enabled the radar to be lowered to a point below the fuselage during flight, offering a 360-degree field of view. These early, rushed prototypes became known as the HAS2(AEW). They were deployed with No 824 NAS on HMS *Illustrious*

Hawker Siddeley Nimrod MR2 XV232, with Avro Shackleton WR963 lurking in the background, at Coventry Airport.

Westland Sea King HC4 ZF122 has recently been returned to the skies by Historic Helicopters.

to the South Atlantic but arrived just after the Argentine surrender. It is felt that if the Royal Navy had had this technology earlier, lives could have been saved. The AEW Sea King programme continued to receive updates and operated successfully for many years until the type's recent retirement in 2018.

Although the Handley Page Victors' defining role in the conflict was air-to-air refuelling, it should be noted that a handful of K2s had cameras and specialised radars refitted in their noses to gather intelligence over the islands. In early April 1982, several crews underwent training in the Maritime Radar Reconnaissance Role over the north coast of Scotland. The converted aircraft also retained their tanking ability too. On 20 April, Victor XL192 established a long-distance reconnaissance flight record, flying over 7,000 miles to conduct a 90-minute radar scan over South Georgia. The flight was supported by two waves of four other Victors to deliver in-flight fuel for the outbound and return journeys. The record would be broken shortly after by the RAF's Nimrods.

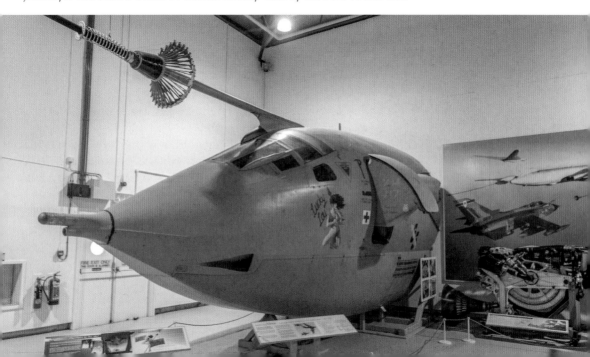

The nose of Handley Page Victor XM717 at the RAF Museum, Hendon – *Lucky Lou* was painted on by Andy Price during the Gulf War.

Sadly, only the nose of Handley Page Victor K2 XM717 has survived; it is now on display at the RAF Museum in Hendon. Although not one of the kitted-out reconnaissance Victors, it did support several surveillance missions as a tanker. On 30 April, it was flown non-stop to Ascension Island, supported and refuelled by another Victor. It was active in the *Black Buck* missions, flying out to support the Vulcan B2 on the night it arrived at Wideawake. It was one of 11 Victors flying that evening – captained by Sqn Ldr B R Neal, it was airborne for over 4 hours. XM717 also supported *Black Buck* missions 2, 5 and 6, as well as providing support for the Harriers on a few occasions and was one of the three Victors refuelling the C1P Hercules airdrop mission on 17 May 1982.

On 15 May 1982, XM717 provided tanking support for a mammoth reconnaissance mission that involved a complex refuelling system, provided by 12 Victors in support of Nimrod MR2P XV232. XM717 was airborne for 3 hours 45 minutes during that mission, whilst the Nimrod achieved a record breaking 19 hours and 5 minutes in the air, covering 8,300 miles. The distance record would be broken by the same aircraft five days later, when XV232 covered 8,453 miles – it remains one of the longest combat sorties ever flown. The mission was flown by pilot Flt Lt Ford and his crew from No 206 Squadron.

Nimrod MR2P XV232 is now in semi-retirement at Coventry Airport and remains live, performing regular engine runs, although proposed developments leave the future of Coventry Airport, and its famous Nimrod and Shackleton uncertain at the time of writing.

Nimrod MR2P XV232 remains live and capable of engine runs at Coventry Airport.

Nimrod MR2 XV226 is kept in ground running condition at Bruntingthorpe Aerodrome. In 1982, XV226 was undergoing upgrade trials from MR1 to MR2 configuration and therefore did not deploy to the South Atlantic.

The Nimrod was developed as a maritime patrol aircraft based on the basic design of the British de Havilland Comet airliner. The Comet was the world's first jet airliner and, after major issues around fatigue and compression were overcome, became a successful aircraft. The de Havilland Aircraft Company began work on the project but, when the company was purchased by Hawker Siddeley in 1960, work on the Nimrod began to gather pace. In 1977, the company merged into British Aerospace, which continued work on the Nimrod.

In the 1960s, the RAF was looking to replace its current maritime patrol aircraft, the Avro Shackleton, with a jet-powered anti-submarine aircraft. The Nimrod MR1 (maritime reconnaissance) was chosen

De Havilland DH-106 Comet 4C XS235, known as *Canopus*, was used as a test bed at Boscombe Down and was the last Comet to fly. It is now kept in running condition at Bruntingthorpe Aerodrome.

as the successor and entered service in 1969. The Shackletons changed roles slightly but remained in service until the 1990s. The Nimrod served until 2010 and, although work was well under way on a vastly improved Nimrod MRA4 to replace it, the project ran into difficulties and was abandoned.

In the spring of 1975, 30 Nimrod MR1s had been selected for upgrading to the MR2 configuration at Woodford. There were several changes made including a new long-range high-resolution EMI Searchwater radar and a new acoustic processor for use with deployed sonobuoys. The upgrade took two years, but, by 1977, the first MR2s were undergoing trials. At this point, the Nimrod lacked air-to-air refuelling capability, but this was hastily added when Argentina invaded the Falklands.

On 5 April 1982, Nimrods were amongst the first British aircraft to arrive on Ascension Island. Initially, they were used to provide patrols around the Island to form an early warning system, as the airfield was being prepared. Nimrods were also deployed to follow the task force as it sailed south, and they were used to relay communications in support of Operation *Black Buck*. Complex refuelling was required to keep the aircraft airborne and that, therefore, limited what it could do over the remote Falkland Islands, but the Nimrods were called upon during large, planned missions to provide search and rescue cover in case of any incidents.

Nimrod MR2 XV250 was converted from an MR1 to an MR2 variant in June 1982, making its first flight in this configuration in 1983. It remains capable of ground running at the Yorkshire Air Museum today.

The RAF also operated a small number of the Nimrod R1s. This was designed to gather electronic signals intelligence in a role known as electronic intelligence gathering (ELINT). The Nimrod R1 was configured differently to the MR1. It had a collection of rotating dish aerials in the bomb bay, as well as more dish aerials in the tail cone and at the front of the wings. It required a large crew of up to 25 personnel to operate the ELINT equipment in the fuselage of the aircraft (as can be seen in these internal images). The Nimrod R1 also required two pilots, a flight engineer and a navigator. The crews would have had to work very closely and get along well together during the 19-hour missions.

To operate in the Falklands theatre, the Nimrod fleet was given some additional modifications. In addition to the new air-to-air refuelling probes, Nimrods also received some extra fire power in the form of 1,000lb of general-purpose bombs, cluster bombs and AIM9 Sidewinder missiles. The Nimrods were asked to cover a wide field across their missions, and some were required to fly close to the Argentine coast to note the locations of Argentine surface vessels.

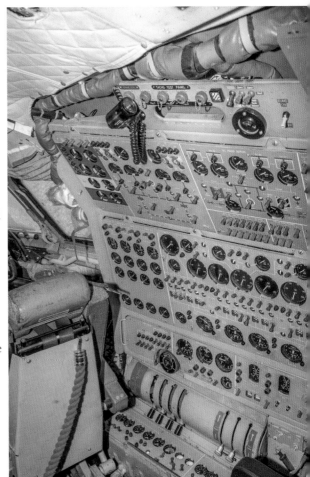

Nimrod R1 XV249 (pictured internally here and externally on the previous page) took its first flight in MR1 configuration on 22 December 1970. It was not changed to R1 configuration until 1995, when XW666, one of the three R1s ditched in the Moray Firth. XV249 was then considered a suitable replacement. In 1982, XV249 was still in MR1 configuration but was flown to Freetown, Sierra Leone, on 1 May 1982 to provide search and rescue cover for the No 1(F) Squadron Harrier GR3s as they deployed to Ascension. It also provided a similar service from Dakar to more Harriers and Phantoms en route from the UK to the South Atlantic. It was also scrambled towards Ascension for a search and rescue call a few months after the war when a Victor tanker had failed to make pre-briefed radio reports. The Victor was found safely 55 miles out but had suffered a radio failure.

In total, 12 Hawker Siddeley Nimrods were deployed to the South Atlantic, made up of the MR1s of No 42 Squadron, the MR2s of Nos 120, 201 and 206 squadrons and the three R1s of No 51 Squadron. The combined force of Nimrods flew 111 missions from Ascension Island during Operation *Corporate*.

English Electric Canberra B6(mod) WT333 at Bruntingthorpe Aerodrome, although WT333 remains there, the Cold War jet's fast taxi days are now consigned to history.

In 1982, the RAF's intelligence branch, known as ISTAR (Intelligence, Surveillance, Target Acquisition and Reconnaissance), was based at RAF Wyton near Huntingdon in Cambridgeshire. Its photo reconnaissance was left to the English Electric Canberra PR9s of No 39 Squadron, which was due to be merged into No 1 PRU (Photographic Reconnaissance Unit) at the end of May 1982. Like most of the British military at this time, it did not expect to be called into action prior to the invasion of the Falklands.

The Canberra was the first British jet bomber developed in the late 1940s, in response to an Air Ministry's request to replace the de Havilland Mosquito in 1944. The development of jet engines enabled the Canberra to take a leap forward in capabilities and, when it was introduced in 1951, it quickly broke records; it was the first jet aircraft to fly non-stop over the Atlantic and, in 1957, established a world altitude record of over 70,000 feet. The Canberra was widely used all over the world and was adopted by a host of foreign nations and was built under licence in Australia and the US, where a small number still operate for NASA.

The Canberra severed for over 50 years in Britain before being retired in 2006. The latest variants were considerably improved from its original specifications, but the design proved successful. Although it was soon replaced by the V-force aircraft as a bomber, it found its niche as a high-level photo reconnaissance aircraft and was so widely used that in some conflicts both sides operated them. This was the case in the Falklands War, when Argentina still utilised a fleet of six Canberras in the ground attack/light bombing role against British forces.

Soon after the Argentine invasion, the British military command quickly realised that they would need top notch reconnaissance in order to plan out the strategy to retake the islands. Options were explored to bring the Canberra into the war, and the only solution found was to disguise Canberras in Chilean Air Force colours so that they could operate out of 'neutral' Chile without causing a political issue between their South American neighbours. This was to be known as Operation *Folklore*. Even reaching Chile was challenging for the ageing air frames and they required some hasty modifications to internal fuel tanks to reach their destination.

To avoid routing through some potentially hostile countries, they planned to make a challenging landing on the Pan-American highway to take on board fuel from a waiting Hercules. The mission experienced issues from the start and when the advance part of C-130s ran into paperwork issues on Tahita, the operation was in jeopardy. Additionally, rumours leaked out to the British press of an RAF Phantom deployment to Chile, whilst this was not entirely true, it seemed enough for Operation *Folklore* to be scrubbed. The war would have to be fought without the aid of the Canberras' intelligence gathering capabilities.

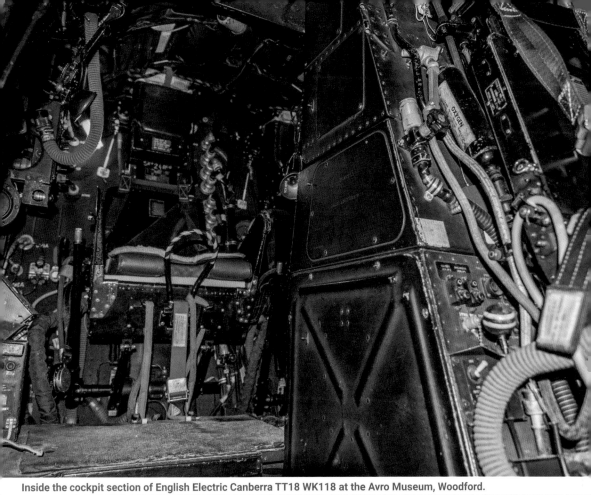

Inside the cockpit section of English Electric Canberra TT18 WK118 at the Avro Museum, Woodford.

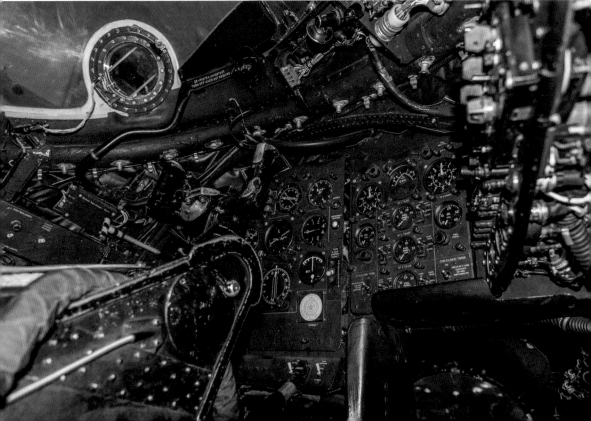

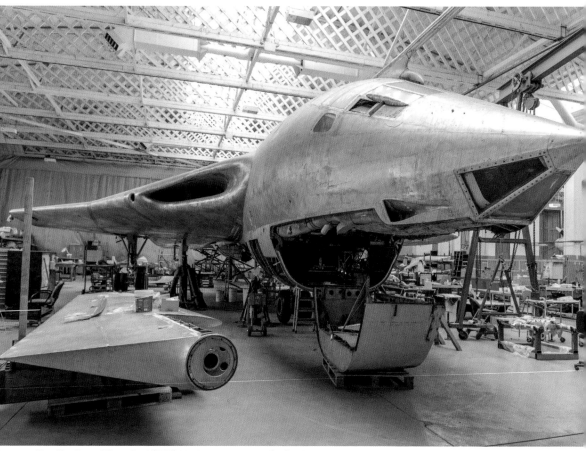

Handley Page Victor B1A(K2P) XH648, at IWM Duxford. When restoration is complete, this will be the only Victor on display that remains in bombing configuration.

became known as the Victor. By 1982, the remaining Victors were converted to tanker aircraft and no longer operated as bombers (see chapter 3).

The final submission was the Avro 698, which in line with the other projects, was given the name Vulcan and, therefore, the combined fleet were referred to as the V-force or V-bombers. The Vulcan was an ambitious attempt to meet the Ministry's specification in full. Roy Chadwick, who had designed the Lancaster bomber, came up with the initial idea to use a delta-wing configuration. Following the German surrender, secret projects had revealed German experimentation with this wing layout, and this may have inspired Chadwick.

After a lengthy development programme, the first production Vulcan took its first flight in 1955 and entered service just over a year later. Forty-five Vulcan B1s were delivered by 1959, all in the anti-flash white paint scheme as their only objective was to deploy nuclear weapons. These first Vulcans were also fitted with air-to-air refuelling systems, which slowly became less important and redundant in the day-to-day role of the bomber. The design of the Vulcan was improved, utilising a new wing shape, a low-level terrain-following radar and more powerful Olympus engines to create the definitive B2 variant. By 1965, 89 Avro Vulcan B2s had entered service with the RAF.

The V-force were designed for one purpose, but fortunately, they were never required to use their nuclear weapons in anger. During the Cold War, the squadrons remained ready to deploy with just four

The last flying Vulcan, XH558, showing its bomb-bays.

minutes' notice. It was considered that by demonstrating that your aircraft could deliver a nuclear weapon, it would act as a deterrent to any would be attacking nation. By the end of the 1960s, the role was handed over to the Royal Navy submarines and the V-bombers were left looking for other employment.

By the 1970s, the Handley Page Victors had all been switched to tanker aircraft and the Vickers Valiant fleet had been retired, leaving the Avro Vulcan as the last large bomber in the RAF. Although the Vulcan had been trialled in other roles like maritime radar reconnaissance and tanking, the Vulcan force remained overall a bombing unit. In the early 1980s, the arrival of new multi-role aircraft, like the Panavia Tornado, heralded the end for the Vulcan. By the beginning of 1982, the last remaining operational Vulcan base, home of Nos 44, 50 and 101 squadrons, at RAF Waddington was well advanced in its preparations to disband.

Wing Commander (Wg Cdr) Simon Baldwin was Officer Commanding No 44 Squadron at the time. He was ordered to put together a plan exploring the possibilities of using the remaining Vulcans to fly operations in the South Atlantic. His first step was to dust off the old in-flight refuelling systems, which had been left forgotten for over a decade. Six aircraft were refitted with the fuelling probes and the crews were instructed to begin air-to-air refuelling practice. Five Vulcans were selected for possible deployment, as these were the only remaining aircraft still fitted with Skybolt missile attachment points and refrigeration ducts. Each Vulcan was also given extra Electronic Counter Measures (ECM) and navigation equipment, including a jamming pod.

Avro Vulcan B2 XL426 is now based at London Southend Airport and is one of only three Vulcans that remains capable of powering up its engines.

Towards the end of April, two Vulcans were prepared for despatch to Wideawake; they were loaded with fuel and 21 1,000lb bombs each. The first target for the Vulcans was Port Stanley airfield, located on the island of East Falkland. This was a prime strategic target, as it was the only airfield on the archipelago capable of operating fast jet aircraft. If the airfield could be put out of service, it would limit Argentina's ability to protect the islands from the air. Air superiority was a pre-requisite for a successful re-invasion via land; the lessons learned from World War Two were still fresh in British military command. At 2250hrs on 30 April 1982, two Avro Vulcan bombers and 11 Handley Page Victor tankers took off at one-minute intervals. The sound of thunder filled the air and Operation *Black Buck* was under way.

Avro Vulcan B2 XM598 (pictured below), piloted by Sqn Ldr John Reeve, was the lead Vulcan. The other Vulcan, XM607, flown by Flt Lt Martin Withers, took off as an airborne spare and was due to return to Ascension Island once the main Vulcan was safely on its way. However, the front window, directly inline of Reeve's vision, failed to seal properly so the crew were unable to pressurise the cabin. The decision was made quickly to return to Wideawake, and XM607 would take its place. On the evening of 3 May, XM598 acted as flying reserve aircraft on *Black Bucks 2*, *5* and *6* and was due to fly lead on the scrubbed *Black Buck 4*. At the end of 1982, XM598 was retired and selected for preservation. It flew into Cosford on 20 January 1983, where it currently takes pride of place in the RAF Museum's National Cold War Exhibition.

In the early hours of the morning on 4 May 1982, the crew of XM607 received the word that they would be flying the mission as the lead aircraft. They were prepared for this eventuality, even if the news did come as a bit of surprise. The refuelling plan was complex, the series of 11 Victor tankers took it in turns to refuel the Vulcan, and each other, at pre-determined points. One by one, the Victors would return to base, with hopefully just enough fuel to get back. The outward journey would require seven fuel transfers to the Vulcan alone. Eventually, the final Vulcan would be left alone for the bombing run before rendezvousing with another outgoing Victor on the way back. Things did not go as smoothly as hoped.

Avro Vulcan B2 XM607 is on the move at RAF Waddington to undergo restoration work on 28 July 2021 – the dignitaries following include *Black Buck 1* pilot Sqn Ldr (then Flt Lt) Martin Withers DFC.

Towards the end of the outbound mission, Sqn Ldr Bob Tuxford in Victor XL189 had refuelled the Vulcan successfully. He was now to pass on fuel to Victor XH669, flown by Ft Lt Steve Biglands, before returning home. As the two tankers were preparing to connect, they suddenly found themselves flying into a raging electrical storm. Although they made contact, the turbulence caused the refuelling probe of XH699 to shear off, and they had no choice but to change place. First, they had to reconnect so Tuxford could take back the fuel he had just passed over. This time it was successful and XH699 returned home.

On the final stage of the outward journey, Vulcan XM607 moved into position behind Victor XL189 and made contact. Flying through the storm had taken up more fuel than expected and Tuxford could not spare as much fuel as Withers and the Vulcan required. In fact, Tuxford had left XL189 short and in

good time would have to call for help, but he maintained radio silence for now. Vulcan XM607 bravely continued to Port Stanley, dropped to bombing altitude and released the 1,000lb bombs diagonally across the airfield, scoring one direct hit on the runway. Success; the code word *Superfuse* was sent, and the Vulcan turned for home in desperate hope of meeting the final Victor in time.

It was a close-run thing, but both the Victor and Vulcan made it back to base safely. Withers was awarded the DFC and Tuxford the Air Force Cross (AFC) for their efforts. A round trip of 7,800 miles made it the longest bombing run in history at that time. Avro Vulcan B2 XM607 would go on to lead further attacks on Port Stanley in *Black Bucks* 2 and 7 and is now preserved as the gate guardian at RAF Waddington. Five out of the seven *Black Buck* missions were completed, they targeted the runway again as well as radar installations and other targets at Port Stanley. None of the other *Black Bucks* achieved the same success as that first mission. The Avro Vulcan had sealed its place in history.

Handley Page Victor K2 XM717 took part in *Black Buck 6* – it is seen here in a fast taxi piloted by Sqn Ldr Bob Tuxford AFC.

Chapter 8

Protection and Ground Attack: RAF Fighter Aircraft

In the late 1970s and early 1980s, the RAF had an impressive collection of high-performance jet fighter aircraft. The planned military strategy during this period was to protect the UK mainland and to support NATO operations in Europe or further afield from fixed forward operating military bases. Aircraft like the SEPECAT Jaguar had an impressive performance with a maximum speed of around 1,000mph, well over the speed of sound. The Jaguar was developed as a joint project between Great Britain and France and was developed for close air support, ground attack and could deliver nuclear weapons. Its range, however, was an issue for operations on a remote island like the Falklands. Its low power cruising range fell well short of the 4,000 miles between Ascension and the Falklands, but at high speeds and combat level, it could only manage around 900 miles. Ironically, the French Air Force planned a naval carrier variant of the Jaguar but opted instead for the Dassault Super Étendard, which was purchased by the Argentine Air Force and used against the British task force. Although superior to the Super Étendard, the Jaguar was not able to contribute to the operations in the South Atlantic.

A collection of SEPECAT Jaguar GR1s under the stars at RAF Cosford.

Blackburn Buccaneer XX900, still capable of engine runs, is now based at Tatenhill Airfield.

The Blackburn (later Hawker Siddeley) Buccaneer was also on strength for the RAF in 1982. It was a supersonic aircraft initially designed as a carrier-based aeroplane for the Royal Navy. It entered FAA service in 1962 but was initially rejected by the RAF. However, when the BAC TSR2 project was cancelled and the purchase of the General Dynamics F-111K fell through, the RAF reluctantly accepted the Buccaneer. During the 1970s, the Royal Navy began a phased retirement of all its larger aircraft carriers, so from 1978, it was unable to effectively operate the Buccaneer, and any remaining airframes were passed on to the RAF. Although this was a carrier-based aircraft, it was unable to operate from any of the remaining smaller carriers left in the Royal Navy, so it did not take part in the Falklands War.

After the BAC TSR2 cancellation and other setbacks in the funding of British projects, the RAF looked to America for a solution. It eventually acquired the impressive McDonell Douglas Phantom II aircraft. The UK was the only country outside of the US to use the Phantom at sea, but by the time of the Falklands War, it was not possible to operate the supersonic jet on the remaining naval aircraft carriers. Options were explored to borrow a large carrier from the US, but this did not come to

McDonell Douglas Phantom FG1 XV582 *Black Mike*, which broke the record for a Lands End to John O'Groats flight on 1 April 1989, at an average speed of over 757mph.

fruition. The British-bought Phantoms were based on the US Navy's F4-J model, only with British avionics and Rolls Royce Spey engines fitted. Two variants of the British Phantom entered service: the FG1 (fighter, ground attack) and the FGR2 (fighter, ground attack, reconnaissance). Although initially planned for these roles, the Phantoms proved so capable that they soon replaced the English Electric Lightnings as the main air defence interceptor protecting the UK.

On 1 April 1982, No 29 (F) Squadron returned from detachment to Cyprus to be greeted by the news that they would be heading out to take part in Operation *Corporate*. The large gathering of military assets on Ascension Island would be a prime target for an aerial attack and therefore needed protection. Three Phantom GR2s (XV466, XV468 and XV484) were deployed to the remote island on 24 May, where they remained on QRA (quick reaction alert) until a month after the Argentine surrender. Prior to this, the QRA duties had been undertaken by the Harriers GR3s of No 1 (F) Squadron. The Phantoms were scrambled on several occasions, including one sortie to intercept two unknown aircraft, which turned out to be Soviet Tu-20 *Bear* aircraft. After the initial deployment, a Phantom presence on Ascension and the Falklands remained for several years after the war. The type was eventually retired from UK service in 1992.

The Hawker Siddeley Harrier GR3s of the RAF's No 1 (F) Squadron were initially deployed as attrition replacements for the Royal Navy's Sea Harriers. However, they were put to good use and found a niche in the low-level ground-attack role. They were also used for low-level reconnaissance missions and for airborne alert sorties. During the retaking of Darwin, Goose Green and the final stages of the conflict, the GR3s proved invaluable in the battlefield air interdiction. This involved strafing and bombing missions in support of the advancing ground forces. It is not an understatement to say that the RAF's GR3s were instrumental in the overall victory.

Harrier GR3 XZ997 (pictured on page 81) was one of five GR3 Harriers to fly non-stop from the UK to Wideawake Airfield on Ascension Island. This was a nine-and-a-half-hour flight that required additional air-to-air refuelling support from Victor tankers. Two days later, XZ997 was on board *Atlantic Conveyor* with five other Harriers en route to the total exclusion zone to join the task force. On 21 May 1982, XZ997 was scheduled to support the initial British landings at San Carlos Water,

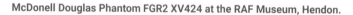

McDonell Douglas Phantom FGR2 XV424 at the RAF Museum, Hendon.

The cockpit of McDonell Douglas Phantom FGR2 XV424.

Harrier GR.3 XZ991, now used by the School of Engineering at RAF Cosford.

however, shortly after launching from HMS *Hermes*, Sqn Ldr Bob Iveson had to abort the mission due to issues with the undercarriage. He landed safely back on *Hermes* after a short 15-minute flight.

Two days later, X7997 was called into action again, this time it joined three other Harriers in a formation attack against the small airstrip at Dunnose Head. The airstrip was not damaged in the attack, but sadly, a nearby local settlement was accidentally hit, causing an injury to a civilian. On 24 May, the Harrier turned its attentions to Port Stanley, however, the 1,000lb bombs had little impact when dropped from low level. The next attack on 28 May by Sqn Ldr Bob Iverson was more successful. The British troops of 2 Para requested air cover and the air-to-ground attack on the gun positions on Goose Green by the Harriers helped instigate the Argentine surrender in this area the following day.

As the British ground forces surged forward, the Harrier GR3s were never far behind. XZ997 was one of a pair of Harriers to fire rockets on defensive forces in the Mount Kent area on 29 May. These missions were followed by another bombing run on the area the following day, but the bombs failed to detonate. On 31 May, another sortie, flown by Flt Lt John Rochfort, aimed for the defences at Port Stanley airport but was hampered by the presence of a forward air controller – a vital link between

the ground forces and air support. Later that day, Flt Lt Mark Hare took XZ997 back to the target, but returned after suffering battle damage from intense small-arms fire.

Bad weather slowed down the intensity of the Harrier operations for several days, but, on 5 June, XZ997 was back in action, this time flown by Wg Cdr Peter Squire, who joined two Sea Harriers in a fruitless search for ground-launched Exocet missiles. On the final few days of the war, XZ997 and the rest of the Harrier fleet continued attacks on the Port Stanley area, as the British ground forces pushed forward. On 13 June, Wg Cdr Peter Squire scored a direct hit on enemy Company HQ on Mount Tumbledown, the first success with laser guided missiles. The next day, XZ997 took off from HMS *Hermes*, flown by Sqn Ldr Peter Harris, for a laser guided bomb attack on Snapper Hill. Before Harris arrived, the white flags were raised in Argentine surrender and the attack was called off.

Harrier GR3 XZ997 remained on the Falklands at the newly named RAF Stanley for a few months after the war, before returning to the UK in October. It served for another nine years in Germany,

the UK and back in the Falklands before being retired to the RAF Museum in 1991. It is currently on display next to fellow Falklands veteran Chinook *Bravo November* at the Cosford site.

Harrier GR3 XZ133 (pictured above and on the previous page) is now based at IWM Duxford, where it hangs from the ceiling in the airspace hangar. On 29 March 1982, it joined No 1 (F) Squadron at RAF Wittering. On 15 April, XZ133 took part in dissimilar air combat training (DACT) out of RAF Binbrook. DACT sorties were used to compare the performances of different aircraft types in preparation for potential conflicts. During this period, trials were undertaken with the French military, as the FAA had purchased several French aircraft types. The knowledge gained from these trials helped prepare Harrier pilots to face the likes of the Argentine Mirages and Super Étendard.

On 28 May 1982, XZ133 was flown from Wittering to St Mawgan before leaving for Wideawake the next day. After just a day's rest, XZ133 was despatched on an 8hr flight to join the task force in the total exclusion zone. It was flown by Flt Lt Murdo MacLeod with the aid of two 100gal ferry fuel tanks that were jettisoned shortly before it embarked onto HMS *Hermes*. XZ133 carried out at least nine attacks against Argentine positions near Stanley and on Mounts Harriet, Longdon and Tumbledown, operating from both HMS *Hermes* and the temporary forward operating strip at Port San Carlos. On 11 June, XZ133 had a lucky escape when an Argentine surface-to-air missile exploded only 100ft above its cockpit during a mission over Mount Longdon. Flt Lt Mike Beech was the fortunate pilot on this occasion.

On 13 June, Flt Lt Mark Hare flew XZ133 alongside Wg Cdr Peter Squire in XZ997 in No 1 (F) Squadron's first successful laser-guided bomb mission, which is discussed on the previous page. On 14 June 1982, Flt Lt Nick Gilchrist took XZ133 into battle one last time. Gilchrist was heading towards the capital, armed with cluster bombs, when the white flags were spotted over Port Stanley. The attack was called off and the war was over. XZ133 remained on the Falkland Islands for several months but was eventually airlifted home in a Chinook after suffering damage when a portable hangar collapsed on top of it during a storm. XZ133 was repaired and put back into operational use, serving throughout the 1980s before eventually being retired to the IWM.

Despite some scepticism before the Falklands War, the Harrier GR3s proved themselves time and again during the conflict. Almost all of the RAF's GR3s took hits from small arms fire at some stage, but the rugged Harrier was able to withstand battle damage. No 1 (F) Squadron also became the first RAF squadron to operate from an aircraft carrier since World War Two and, in the process, proved the RAF's ability to successfully deploy over long distances.

Hawker P1127 XP984 at the Brooklands Museum.

Hawker Kestrel XS695 at the RAF Museum, Cosford.

in the South Atlantic in 1982. The trials also demonstrated to the British government that larger flat-top aircraft carriers fielding McDonnell Douglas F-4 Phantoms, Blackburn Buccaneers and Fairey Gannets were no longer required. British politicians did not anticipate waging a war 8,000 miles from home and, subsequently, the last large aircraft carrier of the Royal Navy, HMS *Ark Royal* was decommissioned in 1978.

The first Sea Harrier, commonly known as the SHAR, entered service with the FAA on 18 June 1979. The arrival of the new aircraft type was not initially welcomed by the pilots, who had just lost their supersonic jets in favour of what they deemed to be a novelty act. After initial training and familiarisation, the FAA pilots started to realise the potential of the Sea Harrier. During trials against the USAF and other friendly, foreign militaries, the Sea Harrier generally achieved a kill ratio of three to one. Pilots even claimed a ratio of ten to one against its predecessor the McDonell Douglas Phantom.

The first variant was the Sea Harrier FRS1 (Fighter, Reconnaissance, Strike), of which 57 were delivered by 1988. The Sea Harrier cemented its

Right and below: Hawker Harrier T Mk 52 G-VTOL at Brooklands Museum.

reputation during the Falklands War. It was fitted with the latest AIM-9 Sidewinder missiles and twin ADEN cannons, as well as a radar system, which made it a potent Combat Air Patrol (CAP) aircraft that protected the task force 24-hours-a-day. By the end of the 74-day war, the Sea Harrier had claimed 20 air-to-air victories without falling victim to enemy aircraft itself. However, six Sea Harriers were lost, two being shot down by ground fire and the other four destroyed in accidents. Through excellent pilots, sound training and good tactics, the Sea Harrier performed admirably, but there were issues to resolve following the war, such as the inability of the Blue Fox radar to see below the aircraft. The lessons learned during the campaign led to an upgrade programme where any survivors were upgraded to FA2 models, which featured more capable Blue Vixen radars and AIM-120 AMRAAM missiles.

Sea Harrier FRS1 XZ493 (pictured opposite) took its first flight in 1980 and entered service with No 801 NAS in January 1981. On 4 April 1982, it set sail from Portsmouth on HMS *Invincible* with another seven serviceable Harriers from the squadron. During the passage, the high visibility blue peace-time paint scheme (that can be seen in the pictures) was replaced with a low-visibility grey scheme, which remained with the Sea Harrier force after the conflict. The Argentine pilots often referred to the Sea Harriers in this guise as La Muerta Negra (The Black Death). The work-up to operational standards began immediately and several training missions were flown by the squadron en route to the South Atlantic.

On 28 August 1982, XZ493 sailed home aboard HMS *Invincible*. It was later upgraded to FA2 configuration but, in 1994, was forced to ditch in the Adriatic Sea whilst operating from HMS *Invincible*. Pilot Lt D Kistruck ejected safely from the aircraft, which was later recovered and restored in its pre-Falklands War paint scheme, as an FRS1 Sea Harrier. It is now on display at the Fleet Air Arm Museum at RNAS Yeovilton.

The Sea Harriers of Nos 800, 801 and 809 NASs provided constant air cover for the task force via a constant series of continuous CAPs. The patrols continued to protect the forces as they landed and progressed forward through the islands. The first air-to-air victory was achieved on 1 May 1982, when Flt Lt Paul Barton of the RAF shot down a Dassault Mirage with a Sidewinder missile. Following this defeat, the Argentines did not further any more of their Mirage fighters in direct assault with the Sea Harriers, instead they kept their most capable interceptor to protect the mainland against a feared Vulcan attack. From then on, only the less capable Skyhawks and Daggers were sent out to attack the British task force directly.

An impressive 50th anniversary celebration of the Harrier at Cosford Air Show in 2019. The evolution is shown by the (from left to right) GR3, T4, Sea Harrier FA2 and GR9 variants.

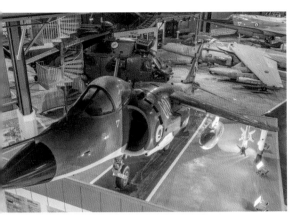

In addition to CAP duties, the Sea Harriers were also used for armed reconnaissance roles and their ability to operate in bad weather and high levels of serviceability meant that the Argentine Air Force could never operate without fear of an encounter with a SHAR. The Sea Harrier operations required a co-ordinated effort from the whole task force. The lack of an EAW aircraft meant that the ships below had to use their radars and communication systems to vector the SHARs onto any would-be targets. Despite its perceived limitations, the Sea Harriers performed their roles incredibly well – the loss of aircraft was less than expected, which freed the GR3s to act as ground-attack aircraft and the CAP Harriers saved the task force shipping on several occasions. Sea Harriers carried out 1,435 missions during the 74-day war, destroyed 20 enemy aircraft in the air, plus three on the ground to just six losses, the additional psychological effect of these successes saved countless British lives by preventing all but the most cautious Argentine attacks.

Chapter 10

Summary

B y 10 June 1982, the British ground forces had successfully landed on East Falkland Island and had pushed the Argentine defences back towards Stanley. The final planned attack to capture the capital was broken into three phases; firstly, they were to take Mount Longdon, Two Sisters and Mount Harriet. Then, the forces would move to Mount Tumbledown and Wireless Ridge, before finally advancing to Snapper Hill. At times the fighting was fierce, but the ground forces continued with gallantry; meanwhile British aircraft were busy overhead.

The stories of the brave sailors at sea and the soldiers on the ground is not covered in this book, but the battles could not have been won without continued air support. Without the large transport aircraft, none of the men, equipment or supplies would have arrived at the islands in time to mount a successful invasion. The data and intelligence gathered by reconnaissance aircraft provided the vital information that was required to plan the attack and adjust strategy as required. The helicopter forces provided a means of ferrying supplies and ammunition and evacuating the injured. Other helicopters supported by the RAF Nimrods also kept the waters free of submarine threats. The Avro Vulcan, with a little help from Handley Page Victor tankers, had taken out the Argentine means of operating fast jets from the islands. Meanwhile, the control of the skies was assured by the superb Sea Harriers on constant CAP. The RAF's GR3 Harriers were frequently called in for ground strikes on heavily protected Argentine defences.

Re-enactor Jed Jaggard wearing period kit next to Falklands veteran Harrier GR3 XZ997.

The record-breaking Nimrod XV232 undergoing a recent engine run at Coventry Airport.

On 14 June 1982, despite having around 8,000 troops in the area, General Menendez had no choice but to surrender to the advancing British ground forces. He had already lost control of the sea and the skies and was left without support. Whilst the whole British task force played their part in the victory, it is fair to say that without the combined effort in the air, the war could not have been won.

During the Falklands War, civil aviation took a back seat on the islands, but it is worth looking at some of the aircraft operating in and around the Falklands during this time period. Stanley Airport was not officially opened until 1979, at which point the islanders could welcome international jet airliners for the first time. When the invasion took place, these international flights were understandably suspended, but they were not actually resumed until 1985. Home-based aircraft (registered as VP-F) were few and far between. The Falkland Islands Government Air Services (FIGAS) provided a vital lifeline to the remote communities spread out on the archipelago, offering postal, transport and air ambulance operations to those in need.

The nose cone of one of the Argentine Daggers shot down by Lt Dave Smith in Sea Harrier ZA193 on 24 May 1982. It is now on display at the Fleet Air Arm Museum

Ex-British Army de Havilland Canada (DHC) Beaver G-DHCZ, similar to the Beavers operated by FIGAS, destroyed during the war.

At the time of the invasion, FIGAS operated a small fleet consisting of Britten Norman Islanders and two de Havilland Canada (DHC) Beavers. On 1 April 1982, one brave pilot planned to set out on a reconnaissance mission to verify the rumours of an Argentine ship in the area. The mission was curtailed as the invasion forces had already arrived before take-off. The FIGAS aircraft were captured and used for Argentine propaganda missions until they were eventually all damaged by British bombing raids. Following the war, a captured Bell UH-1H helicopter was brought back to service by the FIGAS staff, supported by Sea King operative, Lt Cdr R C Cassey of No 820 NAS. This was used to help re-establish the internal air services.

The British Antarctic Survey (BAS) also operated several aircraft that were registered and flown out of the islands in the early 1980s. VP-FAZ, a DHC Twin Otter, was one of those aircraft. It was taken on by the BAS in 1981. At the time of the Argentine invasion, it was actually on board British ship RRS *Bransfield*, which was sailing through Argentine waters but managed to track south and return home safely to the UK around the South Sandwich Islands. VP-FAZ is still operated by the BAS and is registered to the Falkland Islands.

Bell UH-1H helicopter, like the ones in service with Argentina during the conflict.

DHC Twin Otter VP-FAZ of the British Antarctic Survey.

The 74 days of fighting ended on 14 June 1982 when Argentina surrendered, and Britain regained control of the territories. Several British aircraft were lost during the conflict, including three Harrier GR3s, two Sea Harriers, three Gazelles and a Scout all lost in the air, mostly by ground fire. An additional four Sea Harriers, one Harrier GR3, two Wessexes, four Sea Kings and a Scout were lost during flying accidents. The attacks on British shipping also took its toll on the aircraft and three Lynx, three Chinook and seven Wessex helicopters were lost that way. The final lost aircraft of the war was a Westland Sea King, which was destroyed by its crew after a forced landing in Chile during a failed covert mission targeting the Argentine mainland.

Of course, the biggest sacrifice of any war is the loss of human lives: 649 Argentine military personnel, 255 British military personnel, and three Falkland Islanders all paid the ultimate price during the 10-week war. This book is written with the deepest respect to anyone who took part in the conflict, especially those who did not return. Lest we forget.

Below and overleaf: **The Falklands War Memorial at the National Memorial Arboretum in Staffordshire.**

THE FALKLAND ISLANDS
1982

From the Sea – Freedom

APRIL – JUNE 1982
IN HONOUR OF
THE SOUTH ATLANTIC TASK FORCE
AND TO THE ABIDING MEMORY OF THE
255 SAILORS, SOLDIERS AND AIRMEN
WHO GAVE THEIR LIVES AND THOSE WHO
HAVE NO GRAVE BUT THE SEA

Bibliography

Badrocke, Mike, *Avro Vulcan: Owners' Workshop Manual*, Haynes Publishing (2016)

Benson, Harry, *Scram! The gripping first-hand account of the helicopter war in the Falklands*, Preface (2012)

Blackburn, Tony, with Kennedy, Joe, *Nimrod Boys*, Grub Street (2019)

Blackburn, Tony, with O'Keefe, Garry, *Victor Boys*, Grub Street (2007)

Burden, Rodney, Draper, Michael, Rough, Douglas, and Smith, Colin, *Falklands: the Air War*, Arms and Armour Press (1987)

Ellis, Ken, *Wrecks & Relics*, 27th Edition, Crecy Publishing (2020)

Gibson, Chris, *RAF Transport Aircraft*, Key Publishing (2021)

Howard, Lee, *Westland Lynx: Owners' Workshop Manual*, Haynes Publishing (2016)

Howard, Lee, *Westland Wessex: Owners' Workshop Manual*, Haynes Publishing (2018)

Jones, Barry, *British Experimental Turbojet Aircraft*, Crowood Press Ltd (2003)

McNab, Chris, *Falklands War Operations Manual*, Haynes Publishing (2018)

Morgan, David, *Hostile Skies: The Battle for the Falklands*, Cassell (2006)

Sciaroni, Mariano, with Smith, Andy, *Go Find Him and Bring me Back his Hat!: the Royal Navy's Anti-Submarine Campaign in the Falklands/Malvinas War*, Helion & Company Ltd (2020)

Tuxford, Bob, *Contact! A Victor Tanker Captain's Experiences in the RAF Before, During and After the Falklands Conflict,* Grub Street (2016)

White, Rowland, *Harrier 809: Britain's Legendary Jump Jet and the Untold Story of the Falklands War*, Bantam Press (2020)

White, Rowland, *Vulcan 607: the Epic Story of the Most Remarkable Air Attack Since the Second World War*, Bantam Press (2006)

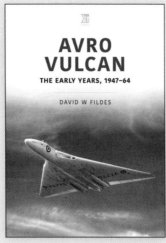
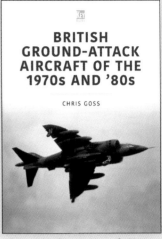